KATE DICAMILLO

Because of
Winn–Dixie

CORNELSEN
ENGLISH
LIBRARY

Cornelsen

CORNELSEN **ENGLISH** LIBRARY
Kate DiCamillo · Because of Winn-Dixie

Verlagsredaktion
Bonnie Glänzer

Annotationen
Birgit Ohmsieder, Berlin
Umschlaggestaltung
hawemannundmosch, Konzeption und Gestaltung, Berlin

Titelbild
Alamy Images, Abingdon: Walter Hodges / Jetta Productions

Gestaltung & technische Umsetzung
Buchgestaltung +, Berlin

www.cornelsen.de
1. Auflage, 7. Druck 2025
Alle Drucke dieser Auflage sind inhaltlich unverändert und können
im Unterricht nebeneinander verwendet werden.
© 2014 Cornelsen Schulverlag GmbH, Berlin
© 2017 Cornelsen Verlag GmbH, Mecklenburgische Str. 53, 14197 Berlin,
E-Mail: service@cornelsen.de

Druck: AZ Druck und Datentechnik GmbH, Kempten
ISBN 978-3-06-033077-5

PEFC-zertifiziert
Dieses Produkt
stammt aus
nachhaltig
bewirtschafteten
Wäldern und
kontrollierten Quellen
PEFC/04-31-2260   www.pefc.de

CONTENTS

My name is India Opal Buloni, and last summer my daddy, the preacher, sent me to the store for a box of macaroni-and-cheese, some white rice and two tomatoes, and I came back with a dog. This is what happened: I walked into the
5 produce section of the Winn-Dixie grocery store to pick out my two tomatoes and I almost bumped right into the store manager. He was standing there all red-faced, screaming and waving his arms around.

"Who let a dog in here?" he kept on shouting. "Who let
10 a dirty dog in here?"

At first, I didn't see a dog. There were just a lot of vegetables rolling around on the floor, tomatoes and onions and green peppers. And there was what seemed like a whole army of Winn-Dixie employees running
15 around waving their arms just the same way the store manager was waving his.

And then the dog came running around the corner. He was a big dog. And ugly. And he looked like he was having a real good time. His tongue was hanging out and he was
20 wagging his tail. He skidded to a stop and smiled right at me. I had never before in my life seen a dog smile, but that is what he did. He pulled back his lips and showed me all his teeth. Then he wagged his tail so hard that he knocked some oranges off a display and they went rolling
25 everywhere, mixing in with the tomatoes and onions and green peppers.

The manager screamed, "Somebody grab that dog!"

The dog went running over to the manager, wagging his tail and smiling. He stood up on his hind legs. You could tell that all he wanted to do was get face to face with the manager and thank him for the good time he was having in the produce department, but somehow he ended up knocking the manager over. And the manager must have been having a bad day because, lying there on the floor, right in front of everybody, he started to cry. The dog leaned over him, real concerned, and licked his face.

"Please," said the manager, "somebody call the pound."

"Wait a minute!" I hollered. "That's my dog. Don't call the pound."

All the Winn-Dixie employees turned around and looked at me, and I knew I had done something big. And maybe stupid, too. But I couldn't help it. I couldn't let that dog go to the pound.

"Here, boy," I said.

The dog stopped licking the manager's face and put his ears up in the air and looked at me, like he was trying to remember where he knew me from.

"Here, boy," I said again. And then I figured that the dog was probably just like everybody else in the world, that he would want to get called by a name, only I didn't know what his name was, so I just said the first thing that came into my head. I said, "Here, Winn-Dixie."

And that dog came trotting over to me just like he had been doing it his whole life.

The manager sat up and gave me a hard stare, like maybe I was making fun of him.

"It's his name," I said. "Honest."

The manager said, "Don't you know not to bring a dog into a grocery store?"

"Yes sir," I told him. "He got in by mistake. I'm sorry. It won't happen again."

"Come on, Winn-Dixie," I said to the dog.

I started walking and he followed along behind me as I went out of the produce department and down the cereal aisle and past all the cashiers and out the door.

5 Once we were safe outside, I checked him over real careful and he didn't look that good. He was big, but skinny; you could see his ribs. And there were bald patches all over him, places where he didn't have any fur at all. Mostly, he looked like a big piece of old brown carpet that
10 had been left out in the rain.

"You're a mess," I told him. "I bet you don't belong to anybody."

He smiled at me. He did that thing again, where he pulled back his lips and showed me his teeth. He smiled so
15 big that it made him sneeze. It was like he was saying, "I know I'm a mess. Isn't it funny?"

It's hard not to immediately fall in love with a dog who has a good sense of humour.

"Come on," I told him. "Let's see what the preacher has
20 to say about you."

And the two of us, me and Winn-Dixie, started walking home.

CHAPTER TWO

That summer I found Winn-Dixie was also the summer me and the preacher moved to Naomi, Florida, so he could be the new preacher at the Open Arms Baptist Church of Naomi. My daddy is a good preacher and a nice man, but
5 sometimes it's hard for me to think about him as my daddy because he spends so much time preaching or thinking about preaching or getting ready to preach. And so, in my mind, I think of him as "the preacher". Before I was born he was a missionary in India and that is how I got my first
10 name. But he calls me by my second name, Opal, because that was his mother's name. And he loved her a lot.

Anyway, while me and Winn-Dixie walked home, I told him how I got my name and I told him how I had just moved to Naomi. I also told him about the preacher and
15 how he was a good man, even if he was too distracted with sermons and prayers and suffering people to go grocery shopping.

"But you know what?" I told Winn-Dixie, "you are a suffering dog, so maybe he will take to you right away.
20 Maybe he'll let me keep you."

Winn-Dixie looked up at me and wagged his tail. He was kind of limping like something was wrong with one of his legs. And I have to admit, he stank. Bad. He was an ugly dog, but already I loved him with all my heart.

25 When we got to the Friendly Corners Trailer Park, I told Winn-Dixie that he had to behave right and be quiet, because this was an all-adult trailer park and the only reason I got to live in it was because the preacher was a preacher and I was a good, quiet kid. I was what the

Friendly Corners Trailer Park manager, Mr Alfred, called "an exception". And I told Winn-Dixie he had to act like an exception, too; specifically, I told him not to pick any fights with Mr Alfred's cats or Mrs Detweller's little yappy Yorkie dog, Samuel. Winn-Dixie looked up at me while I was telling him everything, and I swear he understood.

"Sit," I told him when we got to my trailer. He sat right down. He had good manners. "Stay here," I told him. "I'll be right back."

The preacher was sitting in the living room, working at the little fold-out table. He had papers spread all around him and he was rubbing his nose, which always meant he was thinking. Hard.

"Daddy?" I said.

"Hmmm," he said back.

"Daddy, do you know how you always tell me that we should help those less fortunate than ourselves?"

"Mmmm-hmmm," he said. He rubbed his nose and looked around at his papers.

"Well," I said, "I found a Less Fortunate at the grocery store."

"Is that right?" he said.

"Yes sir," I told him. I stared at the preacher really hard. Sometimes he reminded me of a turtle hiding inside its shell, in there thinking about things and not ever sticking his head out into the world. "Daddy, I was wondering. Could this Less Fortunate, could he stay with us for a while?"

Finally the preacher looked up at me. "Opal," he said, "what are you talking about?"

"I found a dog," I told him. "And I want to keep him."

"No dogs," the preacher said. "We've talked about this before. You don't need a dog."

"I know it," I said. "I know I don't need a dog. But this dog needs me. Look," I said. I went to the trailer door and I hollered, "Winn-Dixie!"

Winn-Dixie's ears shot up in the air and he grinned and sneezed, and then he came limping up the steps and into the trailer and put his head right in the preacher's lap, right on top of a pile of papers.

The preacher looked at Winn-Dixie. He looked at his ribs and his matted-up fur and the places where he was bald. The preacher's nose wrinkled up. Like I said, the dog smelled pretty bad.

Winn-Dixie looked up at the preacher. He pulled back his lips and showed the preacher all of his crooked yellow teeth and wagged his tail and knocked some of the preacher's papers off the table. Then he sneezed and some more papers fluttered to the floor.

"What did you call this dog?" the preacher asked.

"Winn-Dixie," I whispered. I was afraid to say anything too loud. I could see that Winn-Dixie was having a good effect on the preacher. He was making him poke his head out of his shell.

"Well," said the preacher, "he's a stray if ever I've seen one." He put down his pencil and scratched Winn-Dixie behind the ears. "And a Less Fortunate, too. That's for sure. Are you looking for a home?" the preacher asked, real soft, to Winn-Dixie.

Winn-Dixie wagged his tail.

"Well," the preacher said, "I guess you've found one."

CHAPTER THREE

I started in on Winn-Dixie right away, trying to clean him up. First I gave him a bath. I used the garden hose and some baby shampoo. He stood still for it, but I could tell he didn't like it. He looked insulted and the whole time he 5 didn't show me his teeth or wag his tail once. After he was all washed and dried, I brushed him good. I used my own hairbrush and worked real hard at all the knots and patches of fur stuck together. He didn't mind being brushed. He wiggled his back, like it felt pretty good.

10 The whole time I was working on him, I was talking to him. And he listened. I told him how we were alike. "See," I said, "you don't have any family and neither do I. I've got the preacher, of course. But I don't have a mama. I mean, I have one, but I don't know where she is. She left when I 15 was three years old. I can't hardly remember her. And I bet you don't remember your mama much either. So we're almost like orphans."

Winn-Dixie looked straight at me when I said that to him, like he was feeling relieved to finally have somebody 20 understand his situation. I nodded my head at him and went on talking.

"I don't even have any friends, because I had to leave them all behind when we moved here from Watley. Watley's up in north Florida. Have you ever been to north 25 Florida?"

Winn-Dixie looked down at the ground, like he was trying to remember if he had.

"You know what?" I said. "Ever since we moved here, I've been thinking about my mama extra-extra hard, more than I ever did when I was in Watley."

Winn-Dixie twitched his ears and raised his eyebrows.

5   "I think the preacher thinks about my mama all the time, too. He's still in love with her; I know that because I heard the ladies at the church in Watley talking about him. They said he's still hoping she'll come back. But he doesn't tell me that. He won't talk to me about her at all. I want to

10 know more about her. But I'm afraid to ask the preacher; I'm afraid he'll get mad at me."

Winn-Dixie looked at me hard, like he was trying to say something.

"What?" I said.

15 He stared at me.

"You think I should make the preacher tell me about her?"

Winn-Dixie looked at me so hard he sneezed.

"I'll think about it," I said.

20 When I was done working on him, Winn-Dixie looked a whole lot better. He still had his bald spots, but the fur that he did have had cleaned up nice. It was all shiny and soft. You could still see his ribs, but I intended to feed him good and that would take care of that. I couldn't do

25 anything about his crooked yellow teeth because he got into a sneezing fit every time I started brushing them with my toothbrush, and I finally had to give up. But for the most part he looked a whole lot better, and so I took him into the trailer and showed him to the preacher.

30 "Daddy," I said.

"Hmmm," he said. He was working on a sermon and kind of muttering to himself.

"Daddy, I wanted to show you the new Winn-Dixie."

The preacher put down his pencil and rubbed his nose, and finally he looked up.

"Well," he said, smiling real big at Winn-Dixie, "well,
5 now. Don't you look handsome."

Winn-Dixie smiled back at the preacher. He went over and put his head in the preacher's lap.

"He smells nice, too," said the preacher. He rubbed Winn-Dixie's head and looked into his eyes.

10 "Daddy," I said, real quick before I lost all my nerve, "I've been talking to Winn-Dixie."

"Is that right?" the preacher said; he scratched Winn-Dixie's head.

"I've been talking to him and he agreed with me that,
15 since I'm ten years old, you should tell me ten things about my mama. Just ten things, that's all."

The preacher stopped rubbing Winn-Dixie's head and held real still. I could see him thinking about pulling his head back into his shell.

20 "One thing for each year I've been alive," I told him. "Please."

Winn-Dixie looked up at the preacher and kind of gave him a nudge with his nose.

The preacher sighed. He said to Winn-Dixie, "I should
25 have guessed you were going to be trouble." Then he looked at me. "Come on, Opal," he said. "Sit down. And I will tell you ten things about your mama."

CHAPTER FOUR

"One," said the preacher. We were sitting on the couch and Winn-Dixie was sitting between us. Winn-Dixie had already decided that he liked the couch a lot. "One," said the preacher again. Winn-Dixie looked at him kind of
5 hard. "Your mama was funny. She could make just about anybody laugh.

"Two," he said. "She had red hair and freckles."

"Just like me," I said.

"Just like you." The preacher nodded.

10 "Three. She liked to plant things. She had a talent for it. She could stick a tyre in the ground and grow a car."

Winn-Dixie started chewing on his paw, and I tapped him on the head to make him stop.

"Four," said the preacher. "She could run fast. If you
15 were racing her, you couldn't ever let her get a head start, because she would beat you for sure."

"I'm that way, too," I said. "Back home, in Watley, I raced Liam Fullerton, and beat him, and he said it wasn't fair, because boys and girls shouldn't race each other to
20 begin with. I told him he was just a sore loser."

The preacher nodded. He was quiet for a minute.

"I'm ready for number five," I told him.

"Five," he said. "She couldn't cook. She burned everything, including water. She had a hard time opening
25 a can of beans. She couldn't make head nor tail of a piece of meat. Six." The preacher rubbed his nose and looked up at the ceiling. Winn-Dixie looked up, too. "Number six is that your mama loved a story. She would sit and listen to stories all day long. She loved to be told a story. She

especially liked funny ones, stories that made her laugh." The preacher nodded his head like he was agreeing with himself.

"What's number seven?" I asked.

5 "Let's see," he said. "She knew all the constellations, every planet in the night-time sky. Every last one of them. She could name them. And point them out. And she never got tired of looking up at them.

"Number eight," said the preacher, with his eyes closed,
10 "was that she hated being a preacher's wife. She said she just couldn't stand having the ladies at church judge what she was wearing and what she was cooking and how she was singing. She said it made her feel like a bug under a microscope."

15 Winn-Dixie lay down on the couch. He put his nose in the preacher's lap and his tail in mine.

"Ten," said the preacher.

"Nine," I told him.

"Nine," said the preacher. "She drank. She drank beer.
20 And whiskey. And wine. Sometimes she couldn't stop drinking. And that made me and your mama fight quite a bit. Number ten," he said with a long sigh, "number ten is that your mama loved you. She loved you very much."

"But she left me," I told him.

25 "She left us," said the preacher softly. I could see him pulling his old turtle head back into his stupid turtle shell. "She packed her bags and left us, and she didn't leave one thing behind."

"OK," I said. I got up off the couch. Winn-Dixie hopped
30 off, too. "Thank you for telling me," I said.

I went right back to my room and wrote down all ten things that the preacher had told me. I wrote them down just the way he said them to me so that I wouldn't forget them, and then I read them out loud to Winn-Dixie until I had them memorized. I wanted to know those ten things inside and out. That way, if my mama ever came back, I could recognize her, and I would be able to grab her and hold on to her tight and not let her get away from me again.

CHAPTER FIVE

Winn-Dixie couldn't stand to be left alone; we found that out real quick. If me and the preacher went off and left him by himself in the trailer, he pulled all the cushions off the couch and all the toilet paper off the roll. So we started
5 tying him up outside with a rope when we left. That didn't work either. Winn-Dixie howled until Samuel, Mrs Detweller's dog, started howling, too. It was exactly the kind of noise that people in an all-adult trailer park do not like to hear.

10 "He just doesn't want to be left alone," I told the preacher. "That's all. Let's take him with us." I could understand the way Winn-Dixie felt. Getting left behind probably made his heart feel empty.

After a while the preacher gave in. And everywhere we
15 went, we took Winn-Dixie. Even to church.

The Open Arms Baptist Church of Naomi isn't a regular-looking church. The building used to be a Pick-It-Quick store, and when you walk in the front door, the first thing you see is the Pick-It-Quick motto. It's written on the floor
20 in little tiny red tiles that make great big letters that say "PICK PICK PICK QUICK QUICK QUICK". The preacher tried painting over those tiles but the letters won't stay covered up, and so the preacher has just given up and let them be.

25 The other thing about the Open Arms that is different from other churches is there aren't any pews. People bring in their own fold-up chairs and lawn chairs, and so sometimes it looks more like the congregation is watching a parade or sitting at a barbecue instead of being at church.

It's kind of a strange church and I thought Winn-Dixie would fit right in.

But the first time we brought Winn-Dixie to the Open Arms, the preacher tied him outside the front door.

5 "Why did we bring him all the way here just to tie him up?" I asked the preacher.

"Because dogs don't belong in church, Opal," the preacher said. "That's why."

He tied Winn-Dixie to a tree and said how there was 10 lots of shade for him and that it ought to work out real good.

Well, it didn't. The service started and there was some singing and some sharing and some praying, and then the preacher started preaching. And he wasn't but two or 15 three words into his sermon when there was a terrible howl outside.

The preacher tried to ignore it.

"Today," he said.

"Aaaaaarrooo," said Winn-Dixie.

20 "Please," said the preacher.

"Arrrroooowwww," said Winn-Dixie back.

"Friends," said the preacher.

"Arrruiiiiipppp," wailed Winn-Dixie.

Everyone turned in their lawn chairs and fold-up chairs 25 and looked at one another.

"Opal," said the preacher.

"Owwwwww," said Winn-Dixie.

"Yes sir?" I said.

"Go get that dog!" he yelled.

30 "Yes sir!" I yelled back.

I went outside and untied Winn-Dixie and brought him inside, and he sat down beside me and smiled up at the preacher, and the preacher couldn't help it; he smiled back. Winn-Dixie had that effect on him.

And so the preacher started in preaching again. Winn-Dixie sat there listening to it, wiggling his ears this way and that, trying to catch all the words. And everything would have been all right, except that a mouse ran across the floor.

The Open Arms had mice. They were there from when it was a Pick-It-Quick and there were lots of good things to eat in the building, and when the Pick-It-Quick became the Open Arms Baptist Church of Naomi, the mice stayed around to eat all the leftover crumbs from the potluck suppers. The preacher kept on saying he was going to have to do something about them, but he never did. Because the truth is, he couldn't stand the thought of hurting anything, even a mouse.

Well, Winn-Dixie saw that mouse, and he was up and after him. One minute everything was quiet and serious and the preacher was going on and on and on; the next minute Winn-Dixie looked like a furry bullet shooting across the building, chasing that mouse. He was barking and his feet were skidding all over the polished Pick-It-Quick floor, and people were clapping and hollering and pointing. They really went wild when Winn-Dixie actually caught the mouse.

"I have never in my life seen a dog catch a mouse," said Mrs Nordley. She was sitting next to me.

"He's a special dog," I told her.

"I imagine so," she said back.

Winn-Dixie stood up there in front of the whole church, wagging his tail and holding the mouse real careful in his mouth, holding on to him tight but not squishing him.

19

"I believe that mutt has got some retriever in him," said somebody behind me. "That's a hunting dog."

Winn-Dixie took the mouse over to the preacher and dropped it at his feet. And when the mouse tried to get
⁵ away, Winn-Dixie put his paw right on the mouse's tail. Then he smiled up at the preacher. He showed him all his teeth. The preacher looked down at the mouse. He looked at Winn-Dixie. He looked at me. He rubbed his nose. It got real quiet in the Pick-It-Quick.

¹⁰ "Let us pray," the preacher finally said, "for this mouse."

And everybody started laughing and clapping. The preacher picked up the mouse by the tail and walked and threw it out the front door of the Pick-It-Quick, and everybody applauded again.

¹⁵ Then he came back and we all prayed together. I prayed for my mama. I told God how much she would have enjoyed hearing the story of Winn-Dixie catching that mouse. It would have made her laugh. I asked God if maybe I could be the one to tell her that story some day.

²⁰ And then I talked to God about how I was lonely in Naomi because I didn't know that many kids, only the ones from church. And there weren't that many kids at the Open Arms, just Dunlap and Stevie Dewberry, two brothers who weren't twins but looked like they were.
²⁵ And Amanda Wilkinson, whose face was always pinched up like she was smelling something real bad; and Sweetie Pie Thomas, who was only five years old and still mostly a baby. And none of them wanted to be my friend anyway because they probably thought I'd tell on them to the
³⁰ preacher for every little thing they did wrong; and then they would get in trouble with God and their parents. So I told God that I was lonely, even having Winn-Dixie.

And finally I prayed for the mouse, like the preacher suggested. I prayed that he didn't get hurt when he went flying out the door of the Open Arms Baptist Church of Naomi. I prayed that he landed on a nice soft patch of
5 grass.

CHAPTER SIX

I spent a lot of time that summer at the Herman W. Block
Memorial Library. The Herman W. Block Memorial Library
sounds like it would be a big fancy place, but it's not. It's
just a little old house full of books, and Miss Franny Block
5 is in charge of them all. She is a very small, very old woman
with short grey hair, and she was the first friend I made in
Naomi.

It all started with Winn-Dixie not liking it when I went
into the library, because he couldn't go inside, too. But I
10 showed him how he could stand up on his hind legs and
look in the window and see me in there, selecting my
books; and he was OK, as long as he could see me. But the
thing was, the first time Miss Franny Block saw Winn-
Dixie standing up on his hind legs like that, looking in the
15 window, she didn't think he was a dog. She thought he
was a bear.

This is what happened: I was picking out my books and
kind of humming to myself, and all of a sudden there was
this loud and scary scream. I went running up to the front
20 of the library, and there was Miss Franny Block, sitting on
the floor behind her desk.

"Miss Franny?" I said. "Are you all right?"

"A bear," she said.

"A bear?" I asked.

25 "He has come back," she said.

"He has?" I asked. "Where is he?"

"Out there," she said and raised a finger and pointed at
Winn-Dixie standing up on his hind legs, looking through
the window for me.

"Miss Franny Block," I said, "that's not a bear. That's a dog. That's my dog. Winn-Dixie."

"Are you positive?" she asked.

"Yes ma'am," I told her. "I'm positive. He's my dog. I
5 would know him anywhere."

Miss Franny sat there trembling and shaking.

"Come on," I said. "Let me help you up. It's OK." I stuck out my hand and Miss Franny took hold of it, and I pulled her up off the floor. She didn't weigh hardly anything at
10 all. Once she was standing on her feet, she started acting all embarrassed, saying how I must think she was a silly old lady, mistaking a dog for a bear, but that she had a bad experience with a bear coming into the Herman W. Block Memorial Library a long time ago and she never had quite
15 gotten over it.

"When did that happen?" I asked her.

"Well," said Miss Franny, "it is a very long story."

"That's OK," I told her. "I am like my mama in that I like to be told stories. But before you start telling it, can
20 Winn-Dixie come in and listen, too? He gets lonely without me."

"Well, I don't know," said Miss Franny. "Dogs are not allowed in the Herman W. Block Memorial Library."

"He'll be good," I told her. "He's a dog who goes to
25 church." And before she could say yes or no, I went outside and got Winn-Dixie, and he came in and lay down with a "*huummmppff*" and a sigh, right at Miss Franny's feet.

She looked down at him and said, "He most certainly is a large dog."

30 "Yes ma'am," I told her. "He has a large heart, too."

"Well," Miss Franny said. She bent over and gave Winn-Dixie a pat on the head, and Winn-Dixie wagged his tail

23

back and forth and snuffled around her little old-lady feet. "Let me get a chair and sit down so I can tell this story properly."

CHAPTER SEVEN

"Back when Florida was wild, when it consisted of nothing but palmetto trees and mosquitoes so big they could fly away with you," Miss Franny Block started in, "and I was just a little girl no bigger than you, my father, Herman W.
5 Block, told me that I could have anything I wanted for my birthday. Anything at all."

Miss Franny looked around the library. She leaned in close to me. "I don't want to appear prideful," she said, "but my daddy was a very rich man. A very rich man." She
10 nodded and then leaned back and said, "And I was a little girl who loved to read. So I told him, I said, 'Daddy, I would most certainly love to have a library for my birthday; a small little library would be wonderful.'"

"You asked for a whole library?"

15 "A small one." Miss Franny nodded. "I wanted a little house full of nothing but books and I wanted to share them, too. And I got my wish. My father built me this house, the very one we are sitting in now. And at a very young age I became a librarian. Yes ma'am."

20 "What about the bear?" I said.

"Did I mention that Florida was wild in those days?" Miss Franny Block said.

"Uh-huh, you did."

"It was wild. There were wild men and wild women
25 and wild animals."

"Like bears!"

"Yes ma'am. That's right. Now, I have to tell you, I was a little-miss-know-it-all. I was a miss-smarty-pants with my library full of books. Oh, yes ma'am, I thought I knew the answers to everything. Well, one hot Thursday I was sitting in my library with all the doors and windows open and my nose stuck in a book, when a shadow crossed the desk. And without looking up, yes ma'am, without even 5 looking up, I said, 'Is there a book I can help you find?'

"Well, there was no answer. And I thought it might have been a wild man or a wild woman, scared of all these books and afraid to speak up. But then I became aware of a very peculiar smell, a very strong smell. I raised my eyes 10 slowly. And standing right in front of me was a bear. Yes ma'am. A very large bear."

"How big?" I asked.

"Oh, well," said Miss Franny, "perhaps three times the size of your dog."

15 "Then what happened?" I asked her.

"Well," said Miss Franny, "I looked at him and he looked at me. He put his big nose up in the air and sniffed and sniffed as if he was trying to decide if a little-miss-know-it-all librarian was what he was in the mood to eat. 20 And I sat there. And then I thought, well, if this bear intends to eat me, I am not going to let it happen without a fight. No ma'am. So very slowly and very carefully I raised the book I was reading."

"What book was that?" I asked.

25 "Why, it was *War and Peace,* a very large book. I raised it up slowly and then I aimed it carefully and I threw it right at that bear and screamed, 'Be gone!' And do you know what?"

"No ma'am," I said.

30 "He went. But this is what I will never forget. He took the book with him."

"Nuh-uh," I said.

"Yes ma'am," said Miss Franny. "He snatched it up and ran."

"Did he come back?" I asked.

"No, I never saw him again. Well, the men in town used
5 to tease me about it. They used to say, 'Miss Franny, we saw that bear of yours out in the woods today. He was reading that book and he said it sure was good and would it be all right if he kept it for just another week.' Yes ma'am. They did tease me about it." She sighed. "I imagine I'm the
10 only one left from those days. I imagine I'm the only one who even recalls that bear. All my friends, everyone I knew when I was young, they are all dead and gone."

She sighed again. She looked sad and old and wrinkled. It was the same way I felt sometimes, being friendless in a
15 new town and not having a mama to comfort me. I sighed, too.

Winn-Dixie raised his head off his paws and looked back and forth between me and Miss Franny. He sat up then and showed Miss Franny his teeth.

20 "Well now, look at that," she said. "That dog is smiling at me."

"It's a talent of his," I told her.

"It is a fine talent," Miss Franny said. "A very fine talent." And she smiled back at Winn-Dixie.

25 "We could be friends," I said to Miss Franny. "I mean, you and me and Winn-Dixie, we could all be friends."

Miss Franny smiled even bigger. "Why, that would be grand," she said, "just grand."

And right at that minute, right when the three of us
30 had decided to be friends, who should come marching into the Herman W. Block Memorial Library but old pinch-faced Amanda Wilkinson. She walked right up to Miss

Franny's desk and said, "I finished *Johnny Tremain* and I enjoyed it very much. I would like something even more difficult to read now, because I am an advanced reader."

"Yes dear, I know," said Miss Franny. She got up out of
5 her chair.

Amanda pretended like I wasn't there. She stared right past me. "Are dogs allowed in the library?" she asked Miss Franny as they walked away.

"Certain ones," said Miss Franny, "a select few." And
10 then she turned around and winked at me. I smiled back. I had just made my first friend in Naomi, and nobody was going to mess that up for me, not even old pinch-faced Amanda Wilkinson.

CHAPTER EIGHT

Winn-Dixie's bald spots started growing fur, and the fur that he had to begin with started looking shiny and healthy; and he didn't limp any more. And you could tell that he was proud of looking so good, proud of not looking
5 like a stray. I thought what he needed most was a collar and a leash, so I went into Gertrude's Pets, where there were fish and snakes and mice and lizards and gerbils and pet supplies, and I found a real handsome red leather collar with a matching leash.

10 Winn-Dixie was not allowed to come inside the store (there was a big sign on the door that said NO DOGS ALLOWED), so I held the collar and the leash up to the window. And Winn-Dixie, who was standing on the other side of the window, pulled up his lip and showed me his
15 teeth and sneezed and wagged his tail something furious; so I knew he absolutely loved that leash and collar combination. But it was very expensive.

I decided to explain my situation to the man behind the counter. I said, "I don't get a big enough allowance to
20 afford something this fancy. But I love this collar and leash, and so does my dog, and I was thinking that maybe you could set me up on an instalment plan."

"Instalment plan?" said the man.

"Gertrude!" somebody screamed in a real irritating
25 voice.

I looked around. It was a parrot. She was sitting on top of one of the fish tanks, looking right at me.

"An instalment plan," I said, ignoring the parrot, "you know, where I promise to give you my allowance every week and you give me the leash and the collar now."

"I don't think I can do that," said the man. He shook his
5 head. "No, the owner, she wouldn't like that." He looked down at the counter. He wouldn't look at me. He had thick black hair, and it was slicked back like Elvis Presley's. He had on a name tag that said OTIS.

"Or I could work for you," I said. "I could come in and
10 sweep the floors and dust the shelves and take out the trash. I could do that."

I looked around Gertrude's Pets. There was sand and sunflower seed shells and big dust balls all over the floor. I could tell that it needed to be swept.

15 "Uh," said Otis. He looked down at the counter some more.

"Gertrude!" the parrot screamed again.

"I'm real trustworthy," I said. "I'm new in town, but my daddy is a preacher. He's the preacher at the Open Arms
20 Baptist Church of Naomi, so I'm real honest. But the only thing is, Winn-Dixie, my dog, he would have to come inside with me, because if we get separated for too long, he starts to howl something terrible."

"Gertrude doesn't like dogs," said Otis.

25 "Is she the owner?" I asked.

"Yes, I mean, no, I mean . . ." He finally looked up. He pointed at the fish tank. "*That* Gertrude. The parrot. I named her after the owner."

"Gertrude's a pretty bird!" screamed Gertrude.

30 "She might like Winn-Dixie," I told Otis. "Almost everybody does. Maybe he could come inside and meet

30

her, and if the two of them get along, then could I have the job?"

"Maybe," Otis mumbled. He looked down at the counter again.

5   So I went and opened the door, and Winn-Dixie came trotting on inside the store.

"Dog!" screamed Gertrude.

"I know it," Otis told her.

And then Gertrude got real quiet. She sat on the top of 10 the fish tank and cocked her head from one side to the other, looking at Winn-Dixie. And Winn-Dixie stood and stared back at her. He didn't hardly move. He didn't wag his tail. He didn't smile. He didn't sneeze. He just stared at Gertrude and she stared at him. And then she spread her 15 wings out real far and flew and landed on top of Winn-Dixie's head.

"Dog," she croaked.

Winn-Dixie wagged his tail just a little tiny bit.

And Otis said, "You can start on Monday."

20   "Thank you," I told him. "You won't be sorry."

On the way out of Gertrude's Pets, I said to Winn-Dixie, "You are better at making friends than anybody I have ever known. I bet if my mama knew you, she would think you were the best dog ever."

25   Winn-Dixie was smiling up at me and I was smiling down at him, and so neither one of us was looking where we were going and we almost bumped right into Sweetie Pie Thomas. She was standing there, sucking on the knuckle of her third finger, staring in the window of 30 Gertrude's Pets.

She took her finger out of her mouth and looked at me. Her eyes were all big and round. "Was that bird sitting on that dog's head?" she asked. She had her hair tied up in a ponytail with a pink ribbon.

But it wasn't much of a ponytail, it was mostly ribbon and a few strands of hair.

5 "Yes," I told her.

"I seen it," she said. She nodded her head and put her knuckle back in her mouth. Then she took it out again real quick. "I seen that dog in church, too. He was catching a mouse. I want a dog just like it, but my mama won't let me
10 get no dog. She says if I'm real good, I might get to buy me a goldfish or one of them gerbils. That's what she says. Can I pet your dog?"

"Sure," I told her.

Sweetie Pie stroked Winn-Dixie's head so long and
15 serious that his eyes drooped half closed and drool came out of the side of his mouth. "I'm going to be six years old in September. I got to stop sucking on my knuckle once I'm six," said Sweetie Pie. "I'm having a party. Do you want to come to my party? The theme is pink."

20 "Sure," I told her.

"Can this dog come?" she asked.

"You bet," I told her.

And all of a sudden I felt happy. I had a dog. I had a job. I had Miss Franny Block for a friend. And I had my first
25 invitation to a party in Naomi. It didn't matter that it came from a five-year-old and the party wasn't until September. I didn't feel so lonely any more.

CHAPTER NINE

Just about everything that happened to me that summer happened because of Winn-Dixie. For instance, without him I would never have met Gloria Dump. He was the one who introduced us.

5   What happened was this: I was riding my bike home from Gertrude's Pets and Winn-Dixie was running along beside me. We went past Dunlap and Stevie Dewberry's house, and when Dunlap and Stevie saw me, they got on their bikes and started following me. They wouldn't ride
10 with me; they just rode behind me and whispered things that I couldn't hear. Neither one of them had any hair on his head, because their mama shaved their heads every week during the summer because of the one time Dunlap got fleas in his hair from their cat, Sadie. And now they
15 looked like two identical bald-headed babies, even though they weren't twins. Dunlap was ten years old, like me, and Stevie was nine and tall for his age.

"I can hear you," I hollered back at them. "I can hear what you're saying." But I couldn't.

20 Winn-Dixie started to race way ahead of me.

"You better watch out," Dunlap hollered. "That dog is headed right for the witch's house."

"Winn-Dixie," I called. But he kept on going faster and hopped over a gate and went into the most overgrown
25 jungle of a yard that I had ever seen.

"You better go get your dog out of there," Dunlap said.

"The witch will eat that dog," Stevie said.

"Shut up," I told them.

33

I got off my bike and went up to the gate and hollered, "Winn-Dixie, you better come on out of there."

But he didn't.

"She's probably eating him right now," Stevie said. He
5 and Dunlap were standing behind me. "She eats dogs all the time."

"Get lost, you bald-headed babies," I said.

"Hey," said Dunlap, "that ain't a very nice way for a preacher's daughter to talk." He and Stevie backed off a
10 little.

I stood there and thought for a minute. I finally decided that I was more afraid of losing Winn-Dixie than I was of having to deal with a dog-eating witch, so I went through the gate and into the yard.

15 "That witch is going to eat the dog for dinner and you for dessert," Stevie said.

"We'll tell the preacher what happened to you," Dunlap shouted after me.

By then, I was deep in the jungle. There was every kind
20 of thing growing everywhere. There were flowers and vegetables and trees and vines.

"Winn-Dixie?" I said.

"Heh-heh-heh," I heard. "This dog sure likes to eat."

I went around a really big tree all covered in moss, and
25 there was Winn-Dixie. He was eating something right out of the witch's hand. She looked up at me. "This dog sure likes peanut butter," she said. "You can always trust a dog that likes peanut butter."

She was old with crinkly brown skin. She had on a big
30 floppy hat with flowers all over it, and she didn't have any teeth, but she didn't look like a witch. She looked nice. And Winn-Dixie liked her, I could tell.

"I'm sorry he got in your garden," I said.

"You ain't got to be sorry," she said. "I enjoy a little company."

"My name's Opal," I told her.

5   "My name's Gloria Dump," she said. "Ain't that a terrible last name? Dump?"

"My last name is Buloni," I said. "Sometimes the kids at school back home in Watley called me 'Lunch Meat'."

"Hah!" Gloria Dump laughed. "What about this dog? 10 What you call him?"

"Winn-Dixie," I said.

Winn-Dixie thumped his tail on the ground. He tried smiling, but it was hard with his mouth all full of peanut butter.

15   "Winn-Dixie?" Gloria Dump said. "You mean like the grocery store?"

"Yes ma'am," I said.

"Whoooeee," she said. "That takes the strange-name prize, don't it?"

20   "Yes ma'am," I said.

"I was just fixing to make myself a peanut butter sandwich," she said. "You want one, too?"

"All right," I said. "Yes, please."

"Go on and sit down," she said, pointing at a lawn chair 25 with the back all busted out of it. "But sit down careful."

I sat down careful and Gloria Dump made me a peanut butter sandwich on white bread.

Then she made one for herself and put her false teeth in to eat it; when she was done, she said to me, "You know, 30 my eyes ain't too good at all. I can't see nothing but the general shape of things, so I got to rely on my heart. Why

35

don't you go on and tell me everything about yourself, so as I can see you with my heart."

And because Winn-Dixie was looking up at her like she was the best thing he had ever seen, and because the
5 peanut butter sandwich had been so good, and because I had been waiting for a long time to tell some person everything about me, I did.

CHAPTER TEN

I told Gloria Dump everything. I told her how me and the preacher had just moved to Naomi and how I had to leave all my friends behind. I told her about my mama leaving, and I listed the ten things that I knew about her; I explained
5 that here, in Naomi, I missed Mama more than I ever had in Watley. I told her about the preacher being like a turtle, hiding all the time inside his shell. I told her about finding Winn-Dixie in the produce department and how, because of him, I became friends with Miss Franny Block and got a
10 job working for a man named Otis at Gertrude's Pets and got invited to Sweetie Pie Thomas's birthday party. I even told Gloria Dump how Dunlap and Stevie Dewberry called her a witch. But I told her they were stupid, mean, bald-headed boys and I didn't believe them, not for long
15 anyhow.

    And the whole time I was talking, Gloria Dump was listening. She was nodding her head and smiling and frowning and saying, "Hmmm," and "Is that right?"

    I could feel her listening with all her heart, and it felt
20 good.

    "You know what?" she said when I was all done.

    "What?"

    "Could be that you got more of your mama in you than just red hair and freckles and running fast."

25   "Really?" I said. "Like what?"

    "Like maybe you got her green thumb. The two of us could plant something and see how it grows; test your thumb out."

    "OK," I said.

What Gloria Dump picked for me to grow was a tree. Or she said it was a tree. To me, it looked more like a plant. She had me dig a hole for it and put it in the ground and pat the dirt around it tight, like it was a baby and I was 5 tucking it into bed.

"What kind of tree is it?" I asked Gloria Dump.

"It's a wait-and-see tree," she said.

"What's that mean?"

"It means you got to wait for it to grow up before you 10 know what it is."

"Can I come back and see it tomorrow?" I asked.

"Child," she said, "as long as this is my garden, you're welcome in it. But that tree ain't going to have changed much by tomorrow."

15 "But I want to see you, too," I said.

"Hmmmph," said Gloria Dump. "I ain't going nowhere. I be right here."

I woke Winn-Dixie up then. He had peanut butter in his whiskers, and he kept yawning and stretching. He 20 licked Gloria Dump's hand before we left, and I thanked her.

That night when the preacher was tucking me into bed, I told him how I got a job at Gertrude's Pets, and I told him all about making friends with Miss Franny Block and 25 getting invited to Sweetie Pie's party, and I told him about meeting Gloria Dump. Winn-Dixie lay on the floor, waiting for the preacher to leave so he could hop up on the bed like he always did. When I was done talking, the preacher kissed me good night, and then he leaned way over and 30 gave Winn-Dixie a kiss, too, right on top of his head.

"You can go ahead and get up there now," he said to Winn-Dixie.

Winn-Dixie looked at the preacher. He didn't smile at him, but he opened his mouth wide like he was laughing, like the preacher had just told him the funniest joke in the world, and this is what amazed me the most: the preacher
5 laughed back. Winn-Dixie hopped up on the bed, and the preacher got up and turned out the light. I leaned over and kissed Winn-Dixie, too, right on the nose, but he didn't notice. He was already asleep and snoring.

CHAPTER ELEVEN

That night there was a real bad thunderstorm. But what woke me up wasn't the thunder and lightning. It was Winn-Dixie, whining and butting his head against my bedroom door.

5 "Winn-Dixie," I said. "What are you doing?"

He didn't pay any attention to me. He just kept beating his head against the door and whining and whimpering. When I got out of bed and went over and put my hand on his head, he was shaking and trembling so hard that it

10 scared me. I knelt down and wrapped my arms around him, but he didn't turn and look at me or smile or sneeze or wag his tail, or do any normal kind of Winn-Dixie thing; he just kept beating his head against the door and crying and shaking.

15 "You want the door open?" I said. "Huh? Is that what you want?" I stood up and opened the door and Winn-Dixie flew through it like something big and ugly and mean was chasing him.

"Winn-Dixie," I hissed, "come back here." I didn't want

20 him going and waking the preacher up.

But it was too late. Winn-Dixie was already at the other end of the trailer, in the preacher's room. I could tell because there was a *sproi-i-ing* sound that must have come from Winn-Dixie jumping up on the bed, and then there

25 was a sound from the preacher like he was real surprised. But none of it lasted long, because Winn-Dixie came tearing back out of the preacher's room, panting and running like crazy. I tried to grab him, but he was going too fast.

"Opal?" said the preacher. He was standing at the door to his bedroom, and his hair was all kind of wild on top of his head, and he was looking around like he wasn't sure where he was. "Opal, what's going on?"

5 "I don't know," I told him. But just then there was a huge crack of thunder, one so loud that it shook the whole trailer, and Winn-Dixie came shooting back out of my room and went running right past me and I screamed, "Daddy, watch out!"

10 But the preacher was still confused. He just stood there, and Winn-Dixie came barrelling right toward him like he was a bowling ball and the preacher was the only pin left standing, and wham, they both fell to the ground.

"Uh-oh," I said.

15 "Opal?" said the preacher. He was lying on his stomach, and Winn-Dixie was sitting on top of him, panting and whining.

"Yes sir," I said.

"Opal," the preacher said again.

20 "Yes sir," I said louder.

"Do you know what a pathological fear is?"

"No sir," I told him.

The preacher raised a hand. He rubbed his nose. "Well," he said, after a minute, "it's a fear that goes way beyond 25 normal fears. It's a fear you can't be talked out of or reasoned out of."

Just then there was another crack of thunder and Winn-Dixie rose straight up in the air like somebody had poked him with something hot. When he hit the floor, he 30 started running. He ran back to my bedroom and I didn't even try to catch him; I just got out of his way.

The preacher lay there on the ground, rubbing his nose. Finally he sat up. He said, "Opal, I believe Winn-Dixie has a pathological fear of thunderstorms." And just when he finished his sentence, here came Winn-Dixie again, running to save his life. I got the preacher up off the floor and out of the way just in time.

There didn't seem to be a thing we could do for Winn-Dixie to make him feel better, so we just sat there and watched him run back and forth, all terrorized and panting. And every time there was another crack of thunder, Winn-Dixie acted all over again like it was surely the end of the world.

"The storm won't last long," the preacher told me. "And when it's over, the real Winn-Dixie will come back."

After a while the storm did end. The rain stopped. And there wasn't any more lightning, and finally the last rumble of thunder went away and Winn-Dixie quit running back and forth and came over to where me and the preacher were sitting and cocked his head, like he was saying, "What in the world are you two doing out of bed in the middle of the night?"

And then he crept up on the couch with us in this funny way he has, where he gets on the couch an inch at a time, kind of sliding himself onto it, looking off in a different direction, like it's all happening by accident, like he doesn't intend to get on the couch, but all of a sudden, there he is.

And so the three of us sat there. I rubbed Winn-Dixie's head and scratched him behind the ears the way he liked. And the preacher said, "There are an awful lot of thunderstorms in Florida in the summertime."

"Yes sir," I said. I was afraid that maybe he would say we couldn't keep a dog who went crazy with pathological fear every time there was a crack of thunder.

"We'll have to keep an eye on him," the preacher said.
5 He put his arm around Winn-Dixie. "We'll have to make sure he doesn't get out during a storm. He might run away. We have to make sure we keep him safe."

"Yes sir," I said again. All of a sudden it was hard for me to talk. I loved the preacher so much. I loved him because
10 he loved Winn-Dixie. I loved him because he was going to forgive Winn-Dixie for being afraid. But most of all I loved him for putting his arm around Winn-Dixie like that, like he was already trying to keep him safe.

CHAPTER TWELVE

Me and Winn-Dixie got to Gertrude's Pets so early for my
first day of work that the CLOSED sign was still in the
window. But when I pushed on the door it swung open,
and so we went on inside. I was about to call out to Otis
5 that we were there, but then I heard music. It was the
prettiest music I have ever heard in my life. I looked
around to see where it was coming from, and that's when
I noticed that all the animals were out of their cages. There
were rabbits and hamsters and gerbils and mice and birds
10 and lizards and snakes, and they were all just sitting there
on the floor like they had turned to stone, and Otis was
standing in the middle of them. He was playing a guitar
and he had on skinny pointy-toed cowboy boots and he
was tapping them while he was playing the music. His
15 eyes were closed and he was smiling.

Winn-Dixie got a dreamy kind of look on his face. He
smiled really hard at Otis and then he sneezed and then
his whiskers went all fuzzy, and then he sighed and kind of
dropped to the floor with all the other animals. Just then,
20 Gertrude caught sight of Winn-Dixie. "Dog," she croaked,
and flew over and landed on his head. Otis looked up at
me. He stopped playing his guitar and the spell was broken.
The rabbits started hopping and the birds started flying and
the lizards started leaping and the snakes started slithering
25 and Winn-Dixie started barking and chasing everything
that was moving, and Otis shouted, "Help me!"

For what seemed like a long time, me and Otis ran
around trying to catch mice and gerbils and hamsters and
snakes and lizards. We kept on bumping into each other

and tripping over the animals, and Gertrude kept screaming, "Dog! Dog!"

Every time I caught something, I put it back in the first cage I saw; I didn't care if it was the right cage or not. I just put it in and slammed the door. And the whole time I was chasing things, I was thinking that Otis must be some kind of snake charmer, the way he could play his guitar and make all the animals turn to stone. And then I thought, this is silly. I shouted over Winn-Dixie's barking and Gertrude's yelling. I said, "Play some more music, Otis."

He looked at me for a minute. Then he started playing his guitar, and in just a few seconds everything was quiet. Winn-Dixie was lying on the floor, blinking his eyes and smiling to himself and sneezing every now and then, and the mice and the gerbils and the rabbits and the lizards and the snakes that we hadn't caught yet got quiet and sat still, and I picked them up one by one and put them back in their cages.

When I was all done, Otis stopped playing. He looked down at his boots. "I was just playing them some music. It makes them happy."

"Yes sir," I said. "Did they escape from their cages?"

"No," Otis said. "I take them out. I feel sorry for them being locked up all the time. I know what it's like, being locked up."

"You do?" I said.

"I have been in jail," Otis said. He looked up at me real quick and then looked back down at his boots.

"You have?" I said.

"Never mind," said Otis. "Aren't you here to sweep the floor?"

"Yes sir," I told him.

He walked over to the counter and started digging through a pile of things, and finally he came up with a broom.

"Here," he said. "You should start sweeping." Only he must have gotten confused. He was holding out his guitar to me, instead of the broom.

"With your guitar?" I asked.

He blushed and handed me the broom and I started to work. I am a good sweeper. I swept the whole store and then dusted some of the shelves. The whole time I worked, Winn-Dixie followed me, and Gertrude followed him, flying behind him and sitting on his head and his back and croaking real quiet to herself, "Dog, dog."

When I was done, Otis thanked me. I left Gertrude's Pets thinking about how the preacher probably wouldn't like it very much that I was working for a criminal.

Sweetie Pie Thomas was waiting for me right out front. "I seen that," she said. She stood there and sucked on her knuckle and stared at me.

"Seen what?" I said.

"I seen all them animals out of their cages and keeping real still. Is that man magic?" she asked.

"Kind of," I told her.

She hugged Winn-Dixie around the neck. "Just like this grocery-store dog, right?"

"Right," I said.

I started walking, and Sweetie Pie took her knuckle out of her mouth and put her hand in mine.

"Are you coming to my birthday party?" she asked.

"I surely am," I told her.

"The theme is pink," she said.

"I know it," I told her.

"I gotta go," she said all of a sudden. "I gotta go home and tell my mama about what I seen. I live right down there. In that yellow house. That's my mama on the porch. You see her? She's waving at you."

5 I waved at the woman on the porch and she waved back, and I watched Sweetie Pie run off to tell her mama about Otis being a magic man. It made me think about my mama and how I wanted to tell her the story about Otis charming all the animals. I was collecting stories for her. I

10 would also tell her about Miss Franny and the bear, and about meeting Gloria Dump and believing for just a minute that she was a witch. I had a feeling that these were the kind of stories my mama would like, the kind that would make her laugh out loud, the way the preacher said she

15 liked to laugh.

CHAPTER THIRTEEN

Me and Winn-Dixie got into a daily routine where we would leave the trailer early in the morning and get down to Gertrude's Pets in time to hear Otis play his guitar music for the animals. Sometimes Sweetie Pie snuck in for the
5 concert, too. She sat on the floor and wrapped her arms around Winn-Dixie and rocked him back and forth like he was a big old teddy bear. And then when the music was over, she would walk around trying to pick out which pet she wanted; but she always gave up and went home,
10 because the only thing she really wanted was a dog like Winn-Dixie. After she was gone, I would sweep and clean up and even arrange some of Otis's shelves, because he did not have an eye for arranging things and I did. And when I was done, Otis would write down my time in a notebook
15 that he had marked on the outside, "One red leather collar, one red leather leash". And the whole time, he did not in any way ever act like a criminal.

After working at Gertrude's Pets, me and Winn-Dixie would go over to the Herman W. Block Memorial Library
20 and talk to Miss Franny Block and listen to her tell us a story. But my favourite place to be that summer was in Gloria Dump's yard. And I figured it was Winn-Dixie's favourite place to be, too, because when we got up to the last block before her house, Winn-Dixie would break away
25 from my bike and start to run for all he was worth, heading for Gloria Dump's backyard and his spoonful of peanut butter.

Sometimes Dunlap and Stevie Dewberry would follow me. They would holler, "There goes the preacher's daughter, visiting the witch."

"She's not a witch," I told them. It made me mad the
5 way they wouldn't listen to me and kept on believing whatever they wanted to believe about Gloria Dump.

One time Stevie said to me, "My mama says you shouldn't be spending all your time cooped up in that pet shop and at that library, sitting around talking with old
10 ladies. She says you should get out in the fresh air and play with kids your own age. That's what my mama says."

"Oh, lay off her," Dunlap said to Stevie. Then he turned to me. "He don't mean it," he said.

But I was already mad. I shouted at Stevie. I said, "I
15 don't care what your mama says. She's not my mama, so she can't tell me what to do."

"I'm going to tell my mama you said that," shouted Stevie, "and she'll tell your daddy and he'll shame you in front of the whole church. And that pet shop man is
20 retarded and he was in jail and I wonder if your daddy knows that."

"Otis is not retarded," I said. "And my daddy knows that he was in jail." That was a lie. But I didn't care. "And you can go ahead and tell on me if you want, you big bald-
25 headed baby."

I swear, it about wore me out yelling at Dunlap and Stevie Dewberry every day; by the time I got to Gloria Dump's yard I felt like a soldier who had been fighting a hard battle. Gloria would make me a peanut butter
30 sandwich straight off and then she would pour me a cup of coffee with half coffee and half milk and that would refresh me.

"Why don't you play with them boys?" Gloria asked me.

"Because they're ignorant," I told her. "They still think you're a witch. It doesn't matter how many times I tell
5 them you're not."

"I think they are just trying to make friends with you in a roundabout way," Gloria said.

"I don't want to be their friend," I said.

"It might be fun having them two boys for friends."

10 "I'd rather talk with you," I said. "They're stupid. And mean. And they're boys."

Gloria would shake her head and sigh, and then she would ask me what was going on in the world and did I have any stories to tell her. And I always did.

CHAPTER FOURTEEN

Sometimes I told Gloria the story Miss Franny Block had just told me. Or I imitated Otis tapping his pointy-toed boots and playing for all the animals, and that always made her laugh. And sometimes I made up a story and Gloria Dump would listen to it all the way through from beginning to end. She told me she used to love to read stories, but she couldn't any more because her eyes were so bad.

"Can't you get some really strong glasses?" I asked her.

"Child," she said, "they don't make glasses strong enough for these eyes."

One day, when the storytelling was done, I decided to tell Gloria that Otis was a criminal. I thought maybe I should tell an adult about it, and Gloria was the best adult I knew.

"Gloria?" I said.

"Mmmm-hmmm," she said back.

"You know Otis?"

"I don't know him. But I know what you tell me 'bout him."

"Well, he's a criminal. He's been in jail. Do you think I should be afraid of him?"

"What for?"

"I don't know. For doing bad things, I guess. For being in jail."

"Child," said Gloria, "let me show you something." She got up out of her chair real slow and took hold of my arm. "Let's the two of us walk all the way to the back of this yard."

"OK," I said.

We walked and Winn-Dixie followed right behind us. It was a huge yard and I had never been to the back of it. When we got to a big old tree, we stopped.

5 "Look at this tree," Gloria said.

I looked up. There were bottles hanging from just about every branch. There were whiskey bottles and beer bottles and wine bottles all tied on with string, and some of them were clanking against each other and making a spooky
10 kind of noise. Me and Winn-Dixie stood and stared at the tree, and the hair on top of his head rose up a little bit and he growled deep in his throat.

Gloria Dump pointed her cane at the tree.

"What you think about this tree?"

15 I said, "I don't know. Why are all those bottles on it?"

"To keep the ghosts away," Gloria said.

"What ghosts?"

"The ghosts of all the things I done wrong."

I looked at all the bottles on the tree. "You did that
20 many things wrong?" I asked her.

"Mmmm-hmmm," said Gloria. "More than that."

"But you're the nicest person I know," I told her.

"Don't mean I haven't done bad things," she said.

"There's whiskey bottles on there," I told her. "And
25 beer bottles."

"Child," said Gloria Dump, "I know that. I'm the one who put 'em there. I'm the one who drank what was in 'em."

"My mama drank," I whispered.

30 "I know it," Gloria Dump said.

"The preacher says that sometimes she couldn't stop drinking."

52

"Mmmm-hmmm," said Gloria again. "That's the way it is for some folks. We get started and we can't get stopped."

"Are you one of those people?"

"Yes ma'am. I am. But these days I don't drink nothing stronger than coffee."

"Did the whiskey and beer and wine, did they make you do the bad things that are ghosts now?"

"Some of them," said Gloria Dump. "Some of them I would've done anyway, with alcohol or without it. Before I learned."

"Learned what?"

"Learned what is the most important thing."

"What's that?" I asked her.

"It's different for everyone," she said. "You find out on your own. But in the meantime, you got to remember, you can't always judge people by the things they done. You got to judge them by what they are doing now. You judge Otis by the pretty music he plays and how kind he is to them animals, because that's all you know about him right now. All right?"

"Yes ma'am," I said.

"And them Dewberry boys, you try not to judge them too harsh either, all right?"

"All right," I said.

"All right then," said Gloria Dump, and she turned and started walking away. Winn-Dixie nudged me with his wet nose and wagged his tail; when he saw I wasn't going, he trotted after Gloria. I stayed where I was and studied the tree. I wondered if my mama, wherever she was, had a tree full of bottles; and I wondered if I was a ghost to her, the same way she sometimes seemed like a ghost to me.

CHAPTER FIFTEEN

The Herman W. Block Memorial Library's air-conditioning unit didn't work very good, and there was only one fan; and from the minute me and Winn-Dixie got in the library, he hogged it all. He lay right in front of it and wagged his
5 tail and let it blow his fur all around. Some of his fur was pretty loose and blew right off him like a dandelion puff. I worried about him hogging the fan, and I worried about the fan blowing him bald; but Miss Franny said not to worry about either thing, that Winn-Dixie could hog the
10 fan if he wanted and she had never in her life seen a dog made bald by a fan.

Sometimes, when Miss Franny was telling a story, she would have a fit. They were small fits and they didn't last long. But what happened was she would forget what she
15 was saying. She would just stop and start to shake like a little leaf. And when that happened, Winn-Dixie would get up from the fan and sit right at Miss Franny Block's side. He would sit up tall, protecting her, with his ears standing up straight on his head, like soldiers. And when
20 Miss Franny stopped shaking and started talking again, Winn-Dixie would lick her hand and lie back down in front of the fan.

Whenever Miss Franny had one of her fits, it reminded me of Winn-Dixie in a thunderstorm. There were a lot of
25 thunderstorms that summer.

And I got real good at holding on to Winn-Dixie whenever they came. I held on to him and comforted him and whispered to him and rocked him, just the same way he tried to comfort Miss Franny when she had her fits.

Only I held on to Winn-Dixie for another reason, too. I held on to him tight so he wouldn't run away.

It all made me think about Gloria Dump. I wondered who comforted her when she heard those bottles knocking together, those ghosts chattering about the things she had done wrong. I wanted to comfort Gloria Dump. And I decided that the best way to do that would be to read her a book, read it to her loud enough to keep the ghosts away.

And so I asked Miss Franny. I said, "Miss Franny, I've got a grown-up friend whose eyes are going on her, and I would like to read her a book out loud. Do you have any suggestions?"

"Suggestions?" Miss Franny said. "Yes ma'am, I have suggestions. Of course I have suggestions. How about *Gone with the Wind?*"

"What's that about?" I asked her.

"Why," said Miss Franny, "it's a wonderful story about the Civil War."

"The Civil War?" I said.

"Do not tell me you have never heard of the Civil War?" Miss Franny Block looked like she was going to faint. She waved her hands in front of her face.

"I know about the Civil War," I told her. "That was the war between the South and the North over slavery."

"Slavery, yes," said Miss Franny. "It was also about states' rights and money. It was a terrible war. My great-grandfather fought in that war. He was just a boy."

"Your great-grandfather?"

"Yes ma'am, Littmus W. Block. Now *there's* a story."

Winn-Dixie yawned real big and lay down on his side with a thump and a sigh. I swear he knew that phrase:

"Now *there's* a story." And he knew it meant we weren't going anywhere real soon.

"Go ahead and tell it to me, Miss Franny," I said. And I sat down cross-legged next to Winn-Dixie. I pushed him and tried to get him to share the fan. But he pretended he was asleep. And he wouldn't move.

I was all settled in and ready for a good story when the door banged and pinch-faced Amanda Wilkinson came in. Winn-Dixie sat up and stared at her. He tried out a smile on her, but she didn't smile back and so he lay down again.

"I'm ready for another book," Amanda said, slamming her book down on Miss Franny's desk.

"Well," said Miss Franny, "maybe you wouldn't mind waiting. I am telling India Opal a story about my great-grandfather. You are, of course, more than welcome to listen. It will be just one minute."

Amanda sighed a real big dramatic sigh and stared past me. She pretended like she wasn't interested, but she was, I could tell.

"Come sit over here," said Miss Franny.

"I'll stand, thank you," said Amanda.

"Suit yourself." Miss Franny shrugged. "Now where was I? Oh, yes. Littmus. Littmus W. Block."

CHAPTER SIXTEEN

"Littmus W. Block was just a boy when the firing on Fort Sumter occurred," Miss Franny Block said as she started in on her story.

"Fort Sumter?" I said.

5 "It was the firing on Fort Sumter that started the war," said Amanda.

"OK," I said. I shrugged.

"Well, Littmus was fourteen years old. He was strong and big, but he was still just a boy. His daddy, Artley W. 10 Block, had already enlisted, and Littmus told his mama that he could not stand by and let the South get beat, and so he went to fight, too."

Miss Franny looked around the library and then she whispered, "Men and boys always want to fight. They are 15 always looking for a reason to go to war. It is the saddest thing. They have this abiding notion that war is fun. And no history lesson will convince them differently.

"Anyway, Littmus went and enlisted. He lied about his age. Yes ma'am. Like I said, he was a big boy. And the army 20 took him, and Littmus went off to war, just like that. Left behind his mother and three sisters. He went off to be a hero. But he soon found out the truth." Miss Franny closed her eyes and shook her head.

"What truth?" I asked her.

25 "Why, that war is hell," Miss Franny said with her eyes still closed. "Pure hell."

"*Hell* is a cuss word," said Amanda. I stole a look at her. Her face was pinched up even more than usual.

"*War*," said Miss Franny with her eyes still closed, "should be a cuss word, too." She shook her head and opened her eyes. She pointed at me and then she pointed at Amanda. "You, neither of you, can imagine."

5 "No ma'am!" Amanda and me said at exactly the same time. We looked real quick at each other and then back at Miss Franny.

"You cannot imagine. Littmus was hungry all the time. And he was covered with all manner of vermin: fleas and
10 lice. And in the winter, he was so cold he thought for sure he would freeze to death. And in the summer, why there's nothing worse than war in the summertime. It stinks so. And the only thing that made Littmus forget that he was hungry and itchy and hot or cold was that he was getting
15 shot at. And he got shot at quite a bit. And he was nothing more than a child."

"Did he get killed?" I asked Miss Franny.

"Good grief," said Amanda. She rolled her eyes.

"Now, Opal," Miss Franny said, "I wouldn't be standing
20 in this room telling this story if he was killed. I wouldn't exist. No ma'am. He had to live. But he was a changed man. Yes ma'am. A changed man. He walked back home when the war was over. He walked from Virginia all the way back to Georgia. He didn't have a horse. Nobody had
25 a horse except for the Yankees. He walked. And when he got home, there was no home there."

"Where was it?" I asked her. I didn't care if Amanda thought I was stupid. I wanted to know.

"Why," Miss Franny shouted so loud that Winn-Dixie
30 and Amanda Wilkinson and me all jumped, "the Yankees burned it! Yes ma'am. Burned it to the ground."

"What about his sisters?" Amanda asked.

She moved around the desk and came and sat on the floor. She looked up at Miss Franny. "What happened to them?"

"Dead. Dead of typhoid fever."

"Oh no," Amanda said in a real soft voice.

"And his mama?" I whispered.

"Dead, too."

"And his father?" Amanda asked. "What happened to him?"

"He died on the battlefield."

"Littmus was an orphan?" I asked.

"Yes ma'am," said Miss Franny Block. "Littmus was an orphan."

"This is a sad story," I told Miss Franny.

"It sure is," said Amanda. I was amazed that she was agreeing with me about something.

"I am not done yet," Miss Franny said.

Winn-Dixie started to snore, and I nudged him with my foot to try to make him quit. I wanted to hear the rest of the story. It was important to me to hear how Littmus survived after losing everything he loved.

CHAPTER SEVENTEEN

"Well, Littmus came home from the war," said Miss Franny as she went on with her story, "and found himself alone. And he sat down on what used to be the front step of his house, and he cried and cried. He cried just like a baby. He missed his mama and he missed his daddy and he missed his sisters and he missed the boy he used to be. When he finally finished crying, he had the strangest sensation. He felt like he wanted something sweet. He wanted a piece of candy. He hadn't had a piece of candy in years. And it was right then that he made a decision. Yes ma'am. Littmus W. Block figured the world was a sorry affair and that it had enough ugly things in it and what he was going to do was concentrate on putting something sweet in it. He got up and started walking. He walked all the way to Florida. And the whole time he was walking, he was planning."

"Planning what?" I asked.

"Why, planning the candy factory."

"Did he build it?" I asked.

"Of course he did. It's still standing out on Fairville Road."

"That old building?" said Amanda. "That big spooky one?"

"It is not spooky," said Miss Franny. "It was the birthplace of the family fortune. It was there that my great-grandfather manufactured the Littmus Lozenge, a candy that was famous the world over."

"I've never heard of it," said Amanda.

"Me neither," I said.

60

"Well," said Miss Franny, "they aren't made any more. The world, it seems, lost its appetite for Littmus Lozenges. But I still happen to have a few." She opened the top drawer of her desk. It was full of candy. She opened the drawer below that. It was full of candy, too. Miss Franny Block's whole desk was full of candy.

"Would you care for a Littmus Lozenge?" she asked Amanda and me.

"Yes, please," said Amanda.

"Sure," I said. "Can Winn-Dixie have one, too?"

"I have never known a dog that cared for hard candy," said Miss Franny, "but he is welcome to try one."

Miss Franny gave Amanda one Littmus Lozenge and me two. I unwrapped one and held it out to Winn-Dixie. He sat up and sniffed it and wagged his tail and took the candy from between my fingers real gentle. He tried to chew on it, and when that didn't work, he just swallowed the whole thing in one big gulp. Then he wagged his tail at me and lay back down.

I ate my Littmus Lozenge slow. It tasted good. It tasted like root beer and strawberry and something else I didn't have a name for, something that made me feel kind of sad. I looked over at Amanda. She was sucking on her candy and thinking hard.

"Do you like it?" Miss Franny asked me.

"Yes ma'am," I told her.

"What about you, Amanda? Do you like the Littmus Lozenge?"

"Yes ma'am," she said. "But it makes me think of things I feel sad about."

I wondered what in the world Amanda Wilkinson had to feel sad about. She wasn't new to town. She had a mama and a daddy. I had seen her with them in church.

"There's a secret ingredient in there," Miss Franny said.

5 "I know it," I told her. "I can taste it. What is it?"

"Sorrow," Miss Franny said. "Not everybody can taste it. Children, especially, seem to have a hard time knowing it's there."

"I taste it," I said.

10 "Me, too," said Amanda.

"Well, then," Miss Franny said, "you've probably both had your share of sadness."

"I had to move away from Watley and leave all my friends," I said. "That is one sadness I have had. And
15 Dunlap and Stevie Dewberry are always picking on me. That's another sadness. And the biggest one, my biggest sadness, is that my mama left me when I was still small. And I can hardly remember her; I keep hoping I'll get to meet her and tell her some stories."

20 "It makes me miss Carson," said Amanda. She sounded like she was going to cry. "I have to go." And she got up and almost ran out of the Herman W. Block Memorial Library.

"Who's Carson?" I asked Miss Franny.

25 She shook her head. "Sorrow," she said. "It is a sorrow-filled world."

"But how do you put that in a piece of candy?" I asked her. "How do you get that taste in there?"

"That's the secret," she said. "That's why Littmus made
30 a fortune. He manufactured a piece of candy that tasted sweet and sad at the same time."

"Can I have a piece to take to my friend Gloria Dump? And another one to take to Otis down at Gertrude's Pets? And one for the preacher? And one for Sweetie Pie, too?"

"You may have as many as you want," said Miss Franny.

5 So I stuffed my pockets full of Littmus Lozenges and I thanked Miss Franny for her story and I checked out *Gone with the Wind* (which was a very big book) and I told Winn-Dixie to get up, and the two of us left and went over to Gloria Dump's. I rode right past the Dewberrys' house.

10 Dunlap and Stevie were playing football in the front yard and I was just getting ready to stick my tongue out at them; but then I thought about what Miss Franny said, about war being hell, and I thought about what Gloria Dump said, about not judging them too hard. And so I just waved

15 instead. They stood and stared at me; but when I was almost all the way past, I saw Dunlap put his hand up in the air and wave back.

"Hey," he hollered. "Hey, Opal."

I waved harder and I thought about Amanda Wilkinson
20 and how it was neat that she liked a good story the same as I did. And I wondered again ... who was Carson?

CHAPTER EIGHTEEN

When we got to Gloria Dump's, I told her I had two surprises for her and asked which one did she want first, the small one or the big one.

"The small one," said Gloria.

5　I handed her the Littmus Lozenge and she moved it around in her hands, feeling it.

"Candy?" she said.

"Yes ma'am," I told her. "It's called a Littmus Lozenge."

"Oh Lord, yes. I remember these candies. My daddy 10　used to eat them." She unwrapped the Littmus Lozenge and put it in her mouth and nodded her head.

"Do you like it?" I asked her.

"Mmmm-hmmm." She nodded her head slowly. "It taste sweet. But it also taste like people leaving."

15　"You mean sad?" I asked. "Does it taste like sorrow to you?"

"That's right," she said. "It taste sorrowful but sweet. Now. What's surprise number two?"

"A book," I said.

20　"A book?"

"Uh-huh," I said. "I'm going to read it out loud to you. It's called *Gone with the Wind*. Miss Franny says it's a great book. It's about the Civil War. Do you know all about the Civil War?"

25　"I have heard it mentioned a time or two," said Gloria, nodding her head and sucking on her Littmus Lozenge.

"It's going to take us a long time to read this book," I told her. "There are one thousand and thirty-seven pages."

"Whoooeee," said Gloria. She leaned back in her chair and crossed her hands on her stomach. "We best get started then."

And so I read the first chapter of *Gone with the Wind* out loud to Gloria Dump. I read it loud enough to keep her ghosts away. And Gloria listened to it good. And when I was done, she said it was the best surprise she had ever had and she couldn't wait to hear chapter two.

That night I gave the preacher his Littmus Lozenge right before he kissed me good night.

"What's this?" he said.

"It's some candy that Miss Franny's great-grandfather invented. It's called a Littmus Lozenge."

The preacher unwrapped it and put it in his mouth, and after a minute he started rubbing his nose and nodding his head.

"Do you like it?" I asked him.

"It has a peculiar flavour..."

"Root beer?" I said.

"Something else."

"Strawberry?"

"That, too. But there's still something else. It's odd."

I could see the preacher getting further and further away. He was hunching up his shoulders and lowering his chin and getting ready to pull his head inside his shell.

"It almost tastes a little melancholy," he said.

"*Melancholy*? What's that?"

"Sad," said the preacher. He rubbed his nose some more. "It makes me think of your mother."

Winn-Dixie sniffed at the candy wrapper in the preacher's hand.

"It tastes sad," he said, and sighed. "It must be a bad batch."

"No," I told him. I sat up in bed. "That's the way it's supposed to taste. Littmus came back from the war and his
5 whole family was dead. His daddy died fighting. And his mama and his sisters died from a disease and the Yankees burned his house down. And Littmus was sad, very sad, and what he wanted more than anything in the whole world was something sweet. So he built a candy factory
10 and made Littmus Lozenges, and he put all the sad he was feeling into the candy."

"My goodness," said the preacher.

Winn-Dixie snuffled the candy wrapper out of the preacher's hand and started chewing on it.

15 "Give me that," I said to Winn-Dixie. But he wouldn't give it up. I had to reach inside his mouth and pull it out. "You can't eat candy wrappers," I told him.

The preacher cleared his throat. I thought he was going to say something important, maybe tell me another thing
20 that he remembered about my mama; but what he said was, "Opal, I had a talk with Mrs Dewberry the other day. She said that Stevie says that you called him a bald-headed baby."

"It's true," I said. "I did. But he calls Gloria Dump a
25 witch all the time, and he calls Otis retarded. And once he even said that his mama said I shouldn't spend all my time with old ladies. That's what he said."

"I think you should apologize," said the preacher.

"Me?" I said.

30 "Yes," he said. "You. You tell Stevie you're sorry if you said anything that hurt his feelings. I'm sure he just wants to be your friend."

"I don't think so," I told him. "I don't think he wants to be my friend."

"Some people have a strange way of going about making friends," he said. "You apologize."

"Yes sir," I said. Then I remembered Carson. "Daddy," I said, "do you know anything about Amanda Wilkinson?"

"What kind of thing?"

"Do you know something about her and somebody named Carson?"

"Carson was her brother. He drowned last year."

"He's dead?"

"Yes," said the preacher. "His family is still suffering a great deal."

"How old was he?"

"Five," said the preacher. "He was only five years old."

"Daddy," I said, "how could you not tell me about something like that?"

"Other people's tragedies should not be the subject of idle conversation. There was no reason for me to tell you."

"It's just that I needed to know," I said. "Because it helps explain Amanda. No wonder she's so pinch-faced."

"What's that?" said the preacher.

"Nothing," I said.

"Good night, India Opal," the preacher said. He leaned over and kissed me, and I smelled the root beer and the strawberry and the sadness all mixed together on his breath. He patted Winn-Dixie on the head and got up and turned off the light and closed the door.

I didn't go to sleep right away. I lay there and thought how life was like a Littmus Lozenge, how the sweet and the sad were all mixed up together and how hard it was to separate them out. It was confusing.

"Daddy!" I shouted.

After a minute, he opened the door and raised his eyebrows at me.

"What was that word you said? The word that meant sad?"

"*Melancholy*," he said.

"*Melancholy*," I repeated. I liked the way it sounded, like there was music hidden somewhere inside it.

"Good night now," the preacher said.

"Good night," I told him back.

I got up out of bed and unwrapped a Littmus Lozenge and sucked on it hard and thought about my mama leaving me. That was a melancholy feeling. And then I thought about Amanda and Carson. And that made me feel melancholy, too. Poor Amanda. And poor Carson. He was the same age as Sweetie Pie. But he would never get to have his sixth birthday party.

CHAPTER NINETEEN

In the morning, me and Winn-Dixie went down to sweep the pet store, and I took a Littmus Lozenge for Otis.

"Is it Halloween?" Otis asked when I handed him the candy.

5 "No," I said. "Why?"

"Well, you're giving me candy."

"It's just a gift," I told him. "For today."

"Oh," said Otis. He unwrapped the Littmus Lozenge and put it in his mouth. And after a minute tears started 10 rolling down his face.

"Thank you," he said.

"Do you like it?" I asked him.

He nodded his head. "It tastes good, but it also tastes a little bit like being in jail."

15 "Gertrude," Gertrude squawked. She picked up the Littmus Lozenge wrapper in her beak and then dropped it and looked around. "Gertrude!" she screamed again.

"You can't have any," I told her. "It's not for birds." Then, real quick, before I lost my nerve, I said, "Otis, what 20 were you in jail for? Are you a murderer?"

"No ma'am," he said.

"Are you a burglar?"

"No ma'am," Otis said again. He sucked on his candy and stared down at his pointy-toed boots.

25 "You don't have to tell me," I said. "I was just wondering."

"I ain't a dangerous man," Otis said, "if that's what you're thinking. I'm lonely. But I ain't dangerous."

"OK," I said. And I went into the back room to get my broom. When I came back out, Otis was standing where I left him, still staring down at his feet.

"It was on account of the music," he said.

5 "What was?" I asked.

"Why I went to jail. It was on account of the music."

"What happened?"

"I wouldn't stop playing my guitar. Used to be I played it on the street and sometimes people would give me 10 money. I didn't do it for the money. I did it because the music is better if someone is listening to it. Anyway, the police came. And they told me to stop it. They said how I was breaking the law, and the whole time they were talking to me, I went right on playing my music. And that 15 made them mad. They tried to put handcuffs on me." He sighed. "I didn't like that. I wouldn't have been able to play my guitar with them things on."

"And then what happened?" I asked him.

"I hit them," he whispered.

20 "You hit the police?"

"Uh-huh. One of them. I knocked him out. Then I went to jail. And they locked me up and wouldn't let me have my guitar. And when they finally let me out, they made me promise I wouldn't never play my guitar on the street 25 again." He looked up at me real quick and then back down at his boots. "And I don't. I only play it in here. For the animals. Gertrude, the human Gertrude, she owns this shop, and she gave me this job when she read about me in the paper and she said it's all right for me to play music for 30 the animals."

"You play your music for me and Winn-Dixie and Sweetie Pie," I said.

"Yeah," he agreed. "But you ain't on the street."

"Thank you for telling me about it, Otis," I said.

"It's all right," he said. "I don't mind."

Sweetie Pie came in and I gave her a Littmus Lozenge, and she spat it right out; she said that it tasted bad. She said that it tasted like not having a dog.

I swept the floor real slow that day. I wanted to keep Otis company. I didn't want him to be lonely. Sometimes it seemed like everybody in the world was lonely. I thought about my mama. Thinking about her was the same as the hole you keep on feeling with your tongue after you lose a tooth. Time after time my mind kept going to that empty spot, the spot where I felt like she should be.

CHAPTER TWENTY

When I told Gloria Dump about Otis and how he got arrested, she laughed so hard she had to grab hold of her false teeth so they wouldn't fall out of her mouth.

"Whoooeee," she said when she was finally done laughing. "That sure is some dangerous criminal."

"He's a lonely man," I told her. "He just wants to play his music for somebody."

Gloria wiped her eyes with the hem of her dress.

"I know it, sugar," she said. "But sometimes things are so sad they get to be funny."

"You know what else?" I said, still thinking about sad things. "That girl I told you about, the pinch-faced one? Amanda? Well, her brother drowned last year. He was only five years old, the same age as Sweetie Pie Thomas."

Gloria stopped smiling. She nodded her head. "I remember hearing about that," she said. "I remember hearing about a little drowned boy."

"That's why Amanda is so pinch-faced," I said. "She misses her brother."

"Most likely," Gloria agreed.

"Do you think everybody misses somebody? Like I miss my mama?"

"Mmmm-hmmm," said Gloria. She closed her eyes. "I believe, sometimes, that the whole world has an aching heart."

I couldn't stand to think about sad things that couldn't be helped any more, so I said, "Do you want to hear some more *Gone with the Wind?*"

"Yes indeed," Gloria said. "I been looking forward to it all day. Let's see what Miss Scarlett is up to now."

I opened up *Gone with the Wind* and started to read, but the whole time I was thinking about Otis, worrying about him not being allowed to play his guitar for people. In the book, Scarlett was looking forward to going to a big barbecue where there was going to be music and foo d. That's how I got the idea.

"That's what we need to do," I said. I slammed the book shut. Winn-Dixie's head shot up from underneath Gloria's chair. He looked around all nervouslike.

"Huh?" said Gloria Dump.

"Have a party," I told her. "We need to have a party and invite Miss Franny Block and the preacher and Otis, and Otis can play his guitar for everybody. Sweetie Pie can come, too. She listens to his music good."

"'We' who?" Gloria asked.

"'We' me and you. We can make some food and have the party right here in your yard."

"Hmmm," said Gloria Dump.

"We could make peanut butter sandwiches and cut them up in triangles to make them look fancy."

"Lord," said Gloria Dump, "I don't know if the whole world likes peanut butter as much as you and me and this dog."

"OK then," I said, "we could make egg salad sandwiches. Adults like those."

"You know how to make egg salad?"

"No ma'am," I said. "I don't have a mama around to teach me things like that. But I bet you know. I bet you could teach me. Please."

"Maybe," said Gloria Dump. She put her hand on Winn-Dixie's head. She smiled at me. I knew she was telling me yes.

"Thank you," I said. I went over and hugged her. I squeezed her hard. Winn-Dixie wagged his tail and tried to get in between the two of us. He couldn't stand being left out of anything.

"It's going to be the best party ever," I told Gloria.

"You got to make me one promise, though," Gloria said.

"All right," I told her.

"You got to invite them Dewberry boys."

"Dunlap and Stevie?"

"Hmmm-mmm, ain't gonna be no party unless you invite them."

"I have to?"

"Yes," said Gloria Dump. "You promise me."

"I promise," I said. I didn't like the idea. But I promised.

I started inviting people right away. I asked the preacher first.

"Daddy," I said.

"Opal?" the preacher said back.

"Daddy, me and Winn-Dixie and Gloria Dump are having a party."

"Well," said the preacher, "that's nice. You have a good time."

"Daddy," I said, "I'm telling you because you're invited."

"Oh," said the preacher. He rubbed his nose. "I see."

"Can you come?" I asked him.

He sighed. "I don't see why not," he said.

Miss Franny Block took to the idea right away.

"A party!" she said, and clapped her hands together.

"Yes ma'am," I told her. "It will be kind of like the barbecue at Twelve Oaks in *Gone with the Wind*. Only it's not going to be as many people, and we're going to serve egg salad sandwiches instead of barbecue."

5 "That sounds lovely," Miss Franny said. And then she pointed at the back of the library and whispered, "Maybe you should ask Amanda, too."

"She probably won't want to come," I said. "She doesn't like me very much."

10 "Ask her and see what she says," Miss Franny whispered.

So I walked to the back of the library and I asked Amanda Wilkinson in my best-manners voice to please come to my party. She looked around all nervous and 15 stuff.

"A party?" she said.

"Yes," I said. "I sure would like it if you could come."

She stared at me with her mouth open. "OK," she said after a minute. "I mean, yes. Thank you. I would love to."

20 And just like I promised Gloria, I asked the Dewberry boys.

"I ain't going to no party at a witch's house," Stevie said.

Dunlap knocked Stevie with his elbow. "We'll come," 25 he said.

"We will not," said Stevie. "That witch might cook us up in her big old witch's pot."

"I don't care if you come or not," I told them. "I'm just asking because I promised I would."

30 "We'll be there," said Dunlap. And he nodded at me and smiled.

Sweetie Pie was very excited when I invited her.

"What's the theme?" she asked.

"Well, there isn't one," I said.

"You got to think of a theme," she told me. She stuck her knuckle in her mouth and then pulled it back out. "It ain't a party without a theme. Is this dog coming?" she asked. She wrapped her arms around Winn-Dixie and squeezed him so hard that his eyes almost popped out of his head.

"Yes," I told her.

"Good," she said. "You could make that the theme. It could be a dog party."

"I'll think about it," I told her.

The last person I asked was Otis. I told him all about the party and that he was invited and he said, "No, thank you."

"Why not?" I asked.

"I don't like parties," said Otis.

"Please," I begged. "It won't be a party unless you come. I'll give you a whole free week of sweeping and arranging and dusting. If you come to the party, that's what I'll do."

"A whole week for free?" Otis said, looking up at me.

"Yes sir," I told him.

"But I don't have to talk to people, right?"

"No sir," I said. "You don't. But bring your guitar. Maybe you could play us some music."

"Maybe," said Otis. He looked down at his boots again real quick, trying to hide his smile.

"Thank you," I told him. "Thank you for deciding to come."

CHAPTER TWENTY-ONE

After I got Otis convinced to come, the rest of getting ready for the party was easy and fun. Me and Gloria decided to have the party at night, when it would be cooler. And the afternoon before, we worked in Gloria's kitchen and made
5 egg salad sandwiches. We cut them up in triangles and cut off the crusts and put little toothpicks with frilly tops in them. Winn-Dixie sat in the kitchen and looked at us the whole time. He kept on wagging his tail.

"That dog thinks we making these sandwiches for him,"
10 said Gloria Dump.

Winn-Dixie showed Gloria all his teeth.

"These ain't for you," she told him.

But when she thought I wasn't looking, she gave Winn-Dixie an egg salad sandwich, without the toothpick.

15 We also made punch. We mixed together orange juice and grapefruit juice and soda in a big bowl. Gloria called it Dump Punch. She said she was world famous for it. But I had never heard of it before.

The last thing we did was decorate the yard all up. I
20 strung pink and orange and yellow crêpe paper in the trees to make it look fancy. We also filled up paper bags with sand and put candles in them, and right before it was time for the party to start, I went around and lit all the candles. It turned Gloria Dump's yard into a fairyland.

25 "Mmmm-hmmm," said Gloria Dump, looking around. "Even somebody with bad eyes can tell it looks good."

It did look pretty. It looked so pretty that it made my heart feel funny, all swollen and full, and I wished desperately that I knew where my mama was so she could come to the party, too.

Miss Franny Block was the first person to arrive. She was wearing a pretty green dress that was all shiny and shimmery. And she had on high-heeled shoes that made her wobble back and forth when she walked. Even when she was standing still, she still kind of swayed, like she was standing on a boat. She was carrying a big glass bowl full of Littmus Lozenges. "I brought a little after-dinner treat," she said, handing the bowl to me.

"Thank you," I said. I put the bowl on the table next to the egg salad sandwiches and the punch. Then I introduced Miss Franny to Gloria, and they shook hands and said polite things to each other.

And then Sweetie Pie's mother came by with Sweetie Pie. Sweetie Pie had a whole handful of pictures of dogs that she had cut out of magazines. "It's to help you with your theme," she said. "You can use them to decorate. I brung tape, too." And she started going around taping the pictures of the dogs to the trees and the chairs and the table.

"She ain't talked about nothing but this party all day long," said her mother. "Can you walk her home when it's over?"

I promised that I would, and then I introduced Sweetie Pie to Miss Franny and to Gloria, and right after that the preacher showed up. He was wearing a coat and tie and looked real serious. He shook Gloria Dump's hand and Miss Franny Block's hand and said how pleased he was to meet them both and how he had heard nothing but good things about both of them. He patted Sweetie Pie on the head and said it was good to see her outside of church.

And the whole time Winn-Dixie was standing right in the middle of everybody, wagging his tail so hard that I thought for sure he would knock Miss Franny right off her high heels.

5　　Amanda Wilkinson came and she had her blonde hair all curled up and she looked shy and not as mean as usual, and I stood real close to her and introduced her to Gloria Dump. I was surprised at how glad I was to see Amanda. And I wanted to tell her I knew about Carson. I wanted to
10　tell her I understood about losing people, but I didn't say anything. I was just extra nice.

We were all standing around smiling at one another and acting kind of nervous, when a real screechy voice said, "Gertrude is a pretty bird."

15　Winn-Dixie's ears went straight up on his head, and he barked once and looked around. I looked, too, but I didn't see Gertrude. Or Otis.

"I'll be right back," I said to everybody. Me and Winn-Dixie went running around to the front of the house. And
20　sure enough, standing there on the sidewalk was Otis. He had his guitar on his back and Gertrude on his shoulder, and in his hands he was holding the biggest jar of pickles I had ever seen in my life.

"Otis," I said to him, "come on around the back, that's
25　where the party is."

"Oh," he said. But he didn't move. He just stood there, holding on to his jar of pickles.

"Dog," screeched Gertrude. She flew off Otis's shoulder and landed on Winn-Dixie's head.

30　"It's all right, Otis," I told him. "It's just a few people, hardly any people at all."

"Oh," said Otis again. He looked around like he was lost. Then he held up the jar of pickles. "I brought pickles," he said.

"I saw them," I said. "It's just exactly what we needed. 5 They will go perfect with the egg salad sandwiches." I talked to him real soft and gentle and low, like he was a wild animal that I was trying to get to take food out of my hand.

He took one tiny step forward.

10 "Come on," I whispered. I started walking and Winn-Dixie followed me. And when I turned around, I saw Otis was following me, too.

CHAPTER TWENTY-TWO

Otis followed me all the way into the backyard, where the party was. Before he could run away, I introduced him to the preacher.

"Daddy," I said, "this is Otis. He's the one who runs
5 Gertrude's Pets. He's the one who plays the guitar so good."

"How do you do?" said the preacher. He stuck his hand out to Otis. And Otis stood there and shuffled his big jar of pickles back and forth, trying to free up a hand to offer back to the preacher. Finally he ended up bending over
10 and setting the jar down on the ground. But when he did that, his guitar slid forward and hit him in the head with a little *boing* sound; Sweetie Pie laughed and pointed at him like he was doing the whole thing on purpose just to amuse her.

15 "Ouch," said Otis. He stood back up and took the guitar off his shoulder and put it down on the ground next to the jar of pickles, and then he wiped his hand on his pants and stuck it out to the preacher, who took it and said, "It sure is a pleasure to shake your hand."

20 "Thank you," said Otis. "I brought pickles."

"I noticed," said the preacher.

After the preacher and Otis were done shaking hands, I introduced Otis to Miss Franny Block and to Amanda.

And then I introduced him to Gloria Dump. Gloria took
25 his hand and smiled at him. And Otis looked right in her eyes and smiled back. He smiled big.

"I brought pickles for your party," Otis told her.

"And I am so glad," she said. "It just ain't a party without pickles."

Otis looked down at his big jar of pickles. His face was all red.

"Opal," said Gloria, "when are them boys getting here?"

"I don't know," I said. I shrugged. "I told them what time we were starting." What I didn't tell her was that they probably weren't coming, because they were afraid to go to a party at a witch's house.

"Well," said Gloria. "We got egg salad sandwiches. We got Dump Punch. We got pickles. We got dog pictures. We got Littmus Lozenges. And we got a preacher, who can bless this party for us."

Gloria Dump looked over at the preacher.

He nodded his head at Gloria and cleared his throat and said, "Dear God, thank you for warm summer nights and candlelight and good food. But thank you most of all for friends. We appreciate the complicated and wonderful gifts you give us in each other. And we appreciate the task you put down before us, of loving each other the best we can, even as you love us. We pray in Christ's name. Amen."

"Amen," said Gloria Dump.

"Amen," I whispered.

"Gertrude," croaked Gertrude.

"Are we fixing to eat now?" Sweetie Pie asked.

"Shhh," said Amanda.

Winn-Dixie sneezed.

There was a far-off rumble of thunder. I thought at first that it was Winn-Dixie's stomach growling.

"It ain't supposed to rain," said Gloria Dump. "They didn't predict no rain."

"This dress is silk," said Miss Franny Block. "I cannot get it wet."

"Maybe we should go inside," said Amanda.
The preacher looked up at the sky.
And just then, the rain came pouring down.

CHAPTER TWENTY-THREE

"Save the sandwiches," Gloria Dump yelled to me. "Save the punch."

"I got my dog pictures," screamed Sweetie Pie. She went running around, tearing them off the trees and the
5 chairs. "Don't worry," she kept shouting. "I got 'em."

I grabbed the platter of egg salad sandwiches and the preacher grabbed the punch, and we ran into the kitchen with them; and when I ran back outside, I saw that Amanda had hold of Miss Franny Block and was helping
10 her into the house. Miss Franny was so teetery in her high heels that the rain would have knocked her right over if Amanda hadn't held on to her.

I grabbed Gloria Dump's arm.

"I'm all right," she said. But she put her hand on my
15 arm and held on to me tight.

I looked around the garden before we left. All the crêpe paper was melted and the candles were out, and then I saw Otis. He was standing there by his jar of pickles, looking down at his feet.

20 "Otis," I hollered at him over the rain, "come on, we're going inside."

When we got in the kitchen, Amanda and Miss Franny were laughing and shaking themselves like dogs.

"What a downpour," said Miss Franny. "Wasn't that
25 something?"

"That came right out of nowhere," said the preacher.

"Whoooeee," said Gloria.

"Dog," squawked Gertrude. I looked at her. She was sitting on the kitchen table. The thunder was really booming and cracking.

"Oh no," I said. I looked around the kitchen.

5 "Don't worry," said Sweetie Pie. "I saved them dog pictures. I got 'em right here." She waved around her wad of magazine pages.

"Where's Winn-Dixie?" I shouted. "I forgot about him. I was just thinking about the party and I forgot about 10 Winn-Dixie. I forgot about protecting him from the thunder."

"Now, Opal," the preacher said, "he's probably right out in the yard, hiding underneath a chair. Come on, you and I will go look."

15 "Hold on," said Gloria Dump, "let me get you a flashlight and some umbrellas."

But I didn't want to wait. I went running out into the yard. I looked under all the chairs and around all the bushes and trees. I called his name real loud. I felt like 20 crying. It was my fault. I was supposed to hold on to him. And I forgot.

"Opal," I heard the preacher call.

I looked up. He was standing on the porch with Gloria. And Dunlap and Stevie Dewberry were standing there, 25 too.

"Your guests are here," the preacher said.

"I don't care," I hollered.

"Come on up here," Gloria Dump said, her voice all hard and serious. She shone her flashlight out at me.

30 I walked up to the porch and she handed me the flashlight. "Tell these boys, 'hey'," she said. "Tell them you

are glad they came and that you will be right back just as soon as you find your dog."

"Hey," I said. "Thank you for coming. I just got to find Winn-Dixie and then I'll be right back."

Stevie stared at me with his mouth wide open.

"You want me to help?" Dunlap asked.

I shook my head. I tried not to cry.

"Come here, child," Gloria Dump said. She reached for me and pulled me close to her and whispered in my ear, "There ain't no way you can hold on to something that wants to go, you understand? You can only love what you got while you got it."

She squeezed me hard.

"Good luck now," she called, as me and the preacher stepped off the porch and out into the rain.

"Good luck," Miss Franny called from the kitchen.

"That dog ain't lost," I heard Sweetie Pie holler to somebody inside. "That dog's too smart to get lost."

I turned around and looked back, and the last thing I saw was the porch light shining on Dunlap Dewberry's bald head. It made me sad, him standing on Gloria's porch, his bald head glowing. Dunlap saw me looking, and he raised up his hand and waved to me. I didn't wave back.

CHAPTER TWENTY-FOUR

Me and the preacher started walking and calling Winn-Dixie's name. I was glad it was raining so hard, because it made it easy to cry. I cried and cried and cried, and the whole time I was calling for Winn-Dixie.

5   "Winn-Dixie," I screamed.

"Winn-Dixie," the preacher shouted. And then he whistled loud and long. But Winn-Dixie didn't show up.

We walked all through town. We walked past the Dewberrys' house and the Herman W. Block Memorial 10 Library and Sweetie Pie's yellow house and Gertrude's Pets. We walked out to the Friendly Corners Trailer Park and looked underneath our trailer. We walked all the way out to the Open Arms Baptist Church of Naomi. We walked past the railroad tracks and right on down Highway 50. 15 Cars were rushing past us and their tail lights glowed red, like mean eyes staring at us.

"Daddy," I said. "Daddy, what if he got run over?"

"Opal," the preacher said. "We can't worry about what might have happened. All we can do is keep looking."

20   We walked and walked. And in my head I started on a list of ten things that I knew about Winn-Dixie, things I could write on big old posters and put up around the neighbourhood, things that would help people look for him.

25   Number one was that he had a pathological fear of thunderstorms.

Number two was he liked to smile, using all his teeth.

Number three was he could run fast.

Number four was that he snored.

Number five was that he could catch mice without squishing them to death.

Number six was he liked to meet people.

Number seven was he liked to eat peanut butter.

5 Number eight was he couldn't stand to be left alone.

Number nine was he liked to sit on couches and sleep in beds.

Number ten was he didn't mind going to church.

I kept on going over and over the list in my head. I
10 memorized it the same way I had memorized the list of ten things about my mama. I memorized it so if I didn't find him, I would have some part of him to hold on to. But at the same time I thought of something I had never thought of before, and that was that a list of things couldn't even
15 begin to show somebody the real Winn-Dixie, just like a list of ten things couldn't ever get me to know my mama. And thinking about that made me cry even more.

Me and the preacher looked for a long time; and finally he said we had to quit.

20 "But Daddy," I said, "Winn-Dixie's out there somewhere. We can't leave him."

"Opal," the preacher said, "we have looked and looked, and there's only so much looking we can do."

"I can't believe you're going to give up," I told him.

25 "India Opal," the preacher said, rubbing his nose, "don't argue with me."

I stood and stared at him. The rain had let up some. It was mostly a drizzle now.

"It's time to head back," the preacher said.

30 "No," I told him. "You go ahead and go, but I'm going to keep on looking."

"Opal," the preacher said in a real soft voice, "it's time to give up."

"You always give up!" I shouted. "You're always pulling your head inside your stupid old turtle shell. I bet you didn't even go out looking for my mama when she left. I bet you just let her run off, too."

"Baby," the preacher said. "I couldn't stop her. I tried. Don't you think I wanted her to stay, too? Don't you think I miss her every day?" He spread his arms out wide and then dropped them to his sides. "I tried," he said. "I tried." Then he did something I couldn't believe.

He started to cry. The preacher was crying.

His shoulders were moving up and down. And he was making snuffly noises. "And don't believe that losing Winn-Dixie doesn't upset me as much as it does you," he said. "I love that dog. I love him, too."

"Daddy," I said. I went and wrapped my arms around his waist. He was crying so hard he was shaking. "It's all right," I told him. "It's OK. Shhh," I said to him like he was a scared little kid. "Everything will be OK."

We stood there hugging and rocking back and forth, and after a while the preacher stopped shaking and I still held on to him; and I finally got the nerve to ask the question I wanted to ask.

"Do you think she's ever going to come back?" I whispered.

"No," the preacher said. "No, I do not. I've hoped and prayed and dreamed about it for years. But I don't think she'll ever come back."

"Gloria says that you can't hold on to anything. That you can only love what you've got while you've got it."

"She's right," the preacher said. "Gloria Dump is right."

"I'm not ready to let Winn-Dixie go," I said. I had forgotten about him for a minute, what with thinking about my mama.

"We'll keep looking," said the preacher. "The two of us will keep looking for him. But do you know what? I just realized something, India Opal. When I told you your mama took everything with her, I forgot one thing, one very important thing that she left behind."

"What?" I asked.

"You," he said. "Thank God your mama left me you." And he hugged me tighter.

"I'm glad I've got you, too," I told him. And I meant it. I took hold of his hand, and we started walking back into town, calling and whistling for Winn-Dixie the whole way.

CHAPTER TWENTY-FIVE

We heard the music before we even got to Gloria Dump's house. We heard it almost a block away. It was guitar-playing and singing and clapping.

"I wonder what's going on?" my father said.

5 We walked up Gloria's sidewalk and around the back, through her yard and into her kitchen, and what we saw was Otis playing his guitar, and Miss Franny and Gloria sitting there smiling and singing, and Gloria holding Sweetie Pie in her lap. Amanda and Dunlap and Stevie 10 were sitting on the kitchen floor, clapping along and having the best possible time. Even Amanda was smiling. I couldn't believe they were so happy when Winn-Dixie was missing.

"We didn't find him," I shouted at them.

15 The music stopped and Gloria Dump looked at me and said, "Child, we know you didn't find him. You didn't find him because he was right here all along."

She took her cane and poked at something under her chair. "Come on out of there," she said.

20 There was a snuffle and a sigh.

"He's asleep," she said. "He's plumb wore out."

She poked around with her cane again. And Winn-Dixie stood up from underneath her chair and yawned.

"Winn-Dixie!" I hollered.

25 "Dog," Gertrude squawked.

Winn-Dixie wagged his tail and showed me all his teeth and sneezed. I went pushing past everybody. I dropped to the floor and wrapped my arms around him.

"Where have you been?" I asked him.

He yawned again.

"How did you find him?" I asked.

"Now there's a story," said Miss Franny. "Gloria, why don't you tell it?"

5 "Well," said Gloria Dump, "we was all just sitting around waiting on you two. And after I convinced these Dewberry boys that I ain't no scary witch all full of spells and potions—"

"She ain't no witch," Stevie said. He shook his bald 10 head. He looked kind of disappointed.

"Naw," said Dunlap. "She ain't. If she was, she would've turned us into toads by now." He grinned.

"I could have told you that she wasn't a witch. Witches don't exist," said Amanda. "They are just myths."

15 "All right now," said Gloria. "What happened was we got through all them witchy things and then Franny said, why don't we have a little music while we wait for those two to get back. And so Otis played his guitar. And whoooeee, there ain't a song he don't know. And if he 20 don't know it, he can pick it up right quick if you hum it to him. He has a gift."

Gloria stopped and smiled over at Otis, and he smiled back. He looked all lit up from the inside.

"Tell what happened," Sweetie Pie said. "Tell about that 25 dog."

"So," said Gloria. "Franny and me, we started thinking about all these songs we knew from when we was girls. We got Otis to play them and we started singing them, teaching the words to these children."

30 "And then somebody sneezed," Sweetie Pie shouted.

"That's right," said Gloria. "Somebody sneezed and it wasn't none of us. So we looked around, wondering who did, thinking that maybe we got us a burglar in the house. We looked around and we didn't see nothing, so we started into singing again. And sure enough, there was another big *achoo*. Sounded like it was coming from my bedroom.

5 So I sent Otis in there. I said, 'Otis, go on in there and see who is sneezing.' So Otis went. And do you know what he found?"

I shook my head.

"Winn-Dixie!" shouted Sweetie Pie.

10 "That dog of yours was all hid underneath my bed, squeezed under there like the world was about to end. But he was smiling like a fool every time he heard Otis play the guitar, smiling so hard he sneezed."

My daddy laughed.

15 "It is true," Miss Franny said.

"It's the truth," said Stevie.

Dunlap nodded and smiled right at me.

"So," Gloria Dump said, "Otis played his guitar right to that dog, and, a little bit at a time, Winn-Dixie came

20 creeping out from underneath the bed."

"He was covered in dust," said Amanda.

"He looked like a ghost," said Dunlap.

"Yeah," said Sweetie Pie, "just like a ghost."

"Mmmm-hmmm," said Gloria. "Looked just like a

25 ghost. Anyway, the storm stopped after a while. And your dog settled in under my chair. And fell asleep. And that's where he's been ever since, just waiting on you to come back and find him."

"Winn-Dixie," I said. I hugged him so tight he wheezed.

30 "We were out there whistling and calling for you and you were right here all along. Thank you," I said to everybody.

"Well," said Gloria Dump. "We didn't do nothin'. We just sat here and waited and sang some songs. We all got to be good friends. Now. The punch ain't nothin' but water and the egg salad sandwiches got tore up by the rain. You got to eat them with a spoon if you want egg salad. But we got pickles to eat. And Littmus Lozenges. And we still got a party going on."

My daddy pulled out a kitchen chair and sat down.

"Otis," he said, "do you know any hymns?"

"I know some," said Otis.

"You hum it," said Miss Franny, nodding her head, "and he can play it."

So my daddy started humming something and Otis started picking it out on his guitar, and Winn-Dixie wagged his tail and lay back down underneath Gloria's chair. I looked around the room at all the different faces, and I felt my heart swell up inside me with pure happiness.

"I'll be back in a minute," I said.

But they were all singing now and laughing, and Winn-Dixie was snoring, so no one heard me.

CHAPTER TWENTY-SIX

Outside, the rain had stopped and the clouds had gone away and the sky was so clear it seemed like I could see every star ever made. I walked all the way to the back of Gloria Dump's yard. I walked back there and looked at her
5 mistake tree. The bottles were quiet; there wasn't a breeze, so they were just hanging there. I looked at the tree and then I looked up at the sky.

"Mama," I said, just like she was standing right beside me, "I know ten things about you, and that's not enough,
10 that's not near enough. But Daddy is going to tell me more; I know he will, now that he knows you're not coming back. He misses you and I miss you, but my heart doesn't feel empty any more. It's full all the way up. I'll still think about you, I promise. But probably not as much as I did
15 this summer."

That's what I said that night underneath Gloria Dump's mistake tree. And after I was done saying it, I stood just staring up at the sky, looking at the constellations and planets. And then I remembered my own tree, the one
20 Gloria had helped me plant. I hadn't looked at it for a long time. I went crawling around on my hands and knees, searching for it. And when I found it, I was surprised at how much it had grown. It was still small. It still looked more like a plant than a tree. But the leaves and the
25 branches felt real strong and good and right. I was down there on my knees when I heard a voice say,

"Are you praying?" I looked up. It was Dunlap. "No," I said. "I'm not praying. I'm thinking." He crossed his arms and looked down at me.

"What about?" he asked.

"All kinds of different things," I said. "I'm sorry that I called you and Stevie bald-headed babies."

"That's all right," he said. "Gloria told me to come out
5 here and get you."

"I told you she wasn't a witch."

"I know it," he said. "I knew it all along. I was just teasing you."

"Oh," I said. I looked at him close. It was hard to see
10 him good in the dark yard.

"Ain't you ever gonna stand up?" he asked.

"Yeah," I said.

And then he surprised me. He did something I never in a million years thought a Dewberry boy would do. He held
15 out his hand to help me up. And I took it. I let him pull me to my feet.

"I'll race you back to the house," Dunlap said. And he started to run.

"OK," I shouted. "But I'm warning you, I'm fast."

20 We ran, and I beat him. I touched the corner of Gloria Dump's house right before he did.

"You shouldn't be running around in the dark," said Amanda. She was standing on the porch, looking at us. "You could trip over something."

25 "Aw, Amanda," said Dunlap, and he shook his head.

"Aw, Amanda," I said, too. And then I remembered Carson and I felt bad for her. I went up on the porch and took hold of her hand and pulled on her. "Come on," I said, "let's go inside."

30 "India Opal," Daddy said when me and Amanda and Dunlap walked in. "Are you here to sing some songs with us?"

"Yes sir," I said. "Only I don't know that many songs."

"We'll teach you," he said. He smiled at me real big. It was a good thing to see.

"That's right," said Gloria Dump. "We will." Sweetie Pie was still sitting in her lap, but her eyes were closed.

"Care for a Littmus Lozenge?" Miss Franny asked, passing me the bowl.

"Thank you," I told her. I took a Littmus Lozenge and unwrapped it and put it in my mouth.

"Do you want a pickle?" Otis asked, holding up his big jar of pickles.

"No, thank you," I said. "Not right now."

Winn-Dixie came out from underneath Gloria Dump's chair. He sat down next to me and leaned into me the same as I was leaning into my daddy. And Amanda stood right there beside me, and when I looked over at her, she didn't look pinch-faced at all to me.

Dunlap cracked his knuckles and said, "Well, are we gonna sing or what?"

"Yeah," Stevie echoed, "Are we gonna sing or what?"

"Let's sing," said Sweetie Pie, opening her eyes and sitting up straight. "Let's sing for the dog."

Otis laughed and strummed his guitar, and the flavour of the Littmus Lozenge opened in my mouth like a flower blooming, all sweet and sad. And then Otis and Gloria and Stevie and Miss Franny and Dunlap and Amanda and Sweetie Pie and my daddy all started to sing a song. And I listened careful, so I could learn it right.

Abbreviations
AE – American English; sb. – somebody; sth. – something;
jm., jn. – jemandem, jemanden; infml – informal (umgangssprachl.)
pl – Plural; fml – formal

A
abiding [ə'baɪdɪŋ] bleibende(r/s),
  dauerhafte(r/s)
account [ə'kaʊnt]: **on account of**
  (fml) wegen
(to) **ache** [eɪk] schmerzen
(to) **admit** [əd'mɪt] zugeben
adult [ə'dʌlt] Erwachsene/r
advanced [əd'vɑːnst]
  fortgeschritten
affair [ə'feə]: **a sorry affair** eine
  traurige Sache
(to) **afford sth.** [ə'fɔːd] sich etwas
  leisten
ain't [eɪnt] *(infml)* = **is not**
air-conditioning ['eəkən,dɪʃənɪŋ]
  Klimaanlage
aisle [aɪl] Gang (im Supermarkt)
alive [ə'laɪv] am Leben sein,
  lebendig
allowance [ə'laʊəns] Taschengeld
(to) **amaze** [ə'meɪz] erstaunen
(to) **amuse** [ə'mjuːz] amüsieren
anyway ['eniweɪ]: **I would've done
  ... anyway** ... hätte ich
  sowieso gemacht
(to) **apologize** [ə'pɒlədʒaɪz] sich
  entschuldigen

(to) **appreciate** [ə'priːʃieɪt]
  schätzen/zu schätzen wissen
(to) **argue** ['ɑːgjuː] sich streiten
awful ['ɔːfl]: **an awful lot** *(infml)*
  ziemlich viel(e)

B
(to) **back off** [,bæk 'ɒf]
  zurückweichen
bald [bɔːld] glatzköpfig
(to) **bang** [bæŋ] (mit der Tür)
  schlagen
barbecue ['bɑːbɪkjuː] Grillfest
(to) **barrel** ['bærəl] *(infml, AE)*
  rasen
batch [bætʃ] Lieferung
battlefield ['bætlfiːld]
  Schlachtfeld
beak [biːk] Schnabel
(to) **behave** [bɪ'heɪv] sich
  benehmen
(to) **bend over** [,bend 'əʊvə] sich
  nach vorne beugen
best-manners [,best'mænəz]
  wohlerzogenste(r/s)
(to) **bet** [bet] wetten
birthplace ['bɜːθpleɪs] Geburtsort
(to) **bless** [bles] segnen
(to) **bloom** [bluːm] erblühen

(to) **blush** [blʌʃ] rot werden
(to) **boom** [buːm] dröhnen
bowl [bəʊl] Schale
branch [brɑːntʃ] Zweig
breeze [briːz] Brise
broom [bruːm] Besen
brung [brʌŋ] *(infml)* = **brought**
bug [bʌg] *(AE)* Käfer
bullet ['bʊlɪt] (Gewehr)Kugel
(to) **bump (into sb.)** [bʌmp] mit
   jm. zusammenstoßen
burglar [bɜːglə] Einbrecher
(to) **burn** [bɜːn] (ver)brennen
busted out [ˌbʌstɪd ˈaʊt]
   herausgebrochen
(to) **butt** [bʌt] anstoßen

C

can [kæn] Dose
candy [kændi] Bonbon
cane [keɪn] (Geh)Stock
care [keə]: **I don't care.** Es ist mir
   egal. **Would you care**
   for …? Möchtest du …?
cashier [kæ'ʃɪə] Kassierer/in
ceiling ['siːlɪŋ] (Zimmer-)Decke
cereal ['sɪərɪəl] Müsli,
   Frühstücksflocken
charge [tʃɑːdʒ]: (to) **be in charge**
   of sth. für etw. verantwortlich
   sein
(to) **charm** [tʃɑːm] beschwören,
   verzaubern
(to) **chase** [tʃeɪs] jagen
(to) **chatter** ['tʃætə] schwatzen
(to) **chew** [tʃuː] kauen
chin [tʃɪn] Kinn

Civil War [ˌsɪvl ˈwɔː] *Bürgerkrieg*
   in den USA (1861–65), in dem
   die Nordstaaten gegen die
   Südstaaten gekämpft haben
(to) **clank** [klæŋk] klirren
collar [kɒlə] Halsband
(to) **comfort sb.** ['kʌmfət] jn.
   trösten
company ['kʌmpəni] Gesellschaft
complicated ['kɒmplɪkeɪtɪd]
   kompliziert
(to) **concentrate** ['kɒnsntreɪt] sich
   konzentrieren
concerned [kən'sɜːnd] besorgt
(to) **confuse** [kənfjuːz] verwirren
congregation [ˌkɒŋgrɪ'geɪʃn]
   Kirchengemeinde
constellation [ˌkɒnstə'leɪʃn]
   Sternenbild
(to) **convince** [kən'vɪns]
   überzeugen
(to) **coop up** [ˌkuːp ˈʌp]
   einsperren
(to) **cover sth. up** [ˌkʌvər ˈʌp]
   etwas bedecken
(to) **crack** [kræk] knacken;
   krachen **crack of thunder**
   Donnerschlag
(to) **crawl** [krɔːl] krauchen
(to) **creep** [kriːp], **crept, crept**
   kriechen
crêpe paper ['kreɪp] Krepppapier
criminal ['krɪmɪnl]
   Verbrecher/in
crinkly ['krɪŋklɪ] faltig
(to) **croak** [krəʊk] krächzen
crooked ['krʊkɪd] schief
cross-legged [ˌkrɒs 'legd] mit
   gekreuzten Beinen

crumb [krʌm] Krümel
crust [krʌst] Kruste
curled [kɜːld] gelockt
cushion ['kʊʃn] Kissen
cuss word ['kʌs ˌwɜːd]
    Schimpfwort

D

dandelion puff
    ['dændɪlaɪən ˌpʌf] Pusteblume
decision [dɪ'sɪʒn] Entscheidung
(to) **decorate** ['dekəreɪt]
    verzieren
desperate ['despərət] verzweifelt
(to) **dig** [dɪg] graben
dirt [dɜːt] Erde
disappointed [ˌdɪsə'pɔɪntɪd]
    enttäuscht
disease [dɪ'ziːz] Krankheit
display [dɪ'spleɪ]
    (Waren)Auslage
distracted [dɪ'stræktɪd] abgelenkt
downpour ['daʊnpɔː] Regenguss
drizzle ['drɪzl] Nieselregen
drool [druːl] Speichel, Sabber
(to) **droop** [druːp] zufallen
(to) **drop** [drɒp] herabsinken
(to) **drown** [draʊn] ertrinken
during ['djʊərɪŋ] während
(to) **dust** [dʌst] Staub wischen
dust ball ['dʌst bɔːl] Wollmaus

E

(to) **echo** ['ekəʊ] wiederholen
elbow ['elbəʊ] Ellenbogen
Elvis Presley [ˌelvɪs 'prezli] *Sänger*
    (1935–1977)

embarrassed [ɪm'bærəst]
    verlegen
employee [ɪm'plɔɪiː] Angestellte/r
empty ['emptɪ] leer
(to) **enlist** [ɪn'lɪst] sich für etwas
    einschreiben, sich freiwillig
    (für die Armee) melden
ever ['evə]: **best ... ever**
    beste (r/s) ... die/den/das es je
    gab
exception [ɪk'sepʃn] Ausnahme
(to) **exist** [ɪg'zɪst] existieren
experience [ɪks'pɪərɪens]
    Erfahrung
eyebrow ['aɪbraʊ]: (to) **raise an**
    eyebrow die Augenbraue
    hochziehen

F

factory ['fæktrɪ] Fabrik
(to) **faint** [feɪnt] in Ohnmacht
    fallen
fairyland ['feərɪlænd]
    Märchenland
fan [fæn] Ventilator
fancy ['fænsi] schick
far-off [ˌfɑːr ‿'ɒf] weit entfernt
fault [fɔːlt] Schuld
(to) **figure** ['fɪgə] sich etwas
    denken
fit [fɪt] Anfall
(to) **fit in** [ˌfɪt 'ɪn] passen
fix [fɪks]: **fixing to do sth.** *(infml,*
    AE) = **going to do sth.**
flashlight ['flæʃlaɪt]
    Taschenlampe
flea [fliː] Floh
floppy hat [ˌflɒpɪ 'hæt]
    Schlapphut

(to) **flutter** ['flʌtə] flattern
(to) **fold** [fəʊld] falten
    fold-out table Klapptisch
    fold-up chair Klappstuhl
fortunate ['fɔ:tʃənət] glücklich
fortune ['fɔ:tʃu:n] Vermögen
    (to) **make a fortune** ein
    Vermögen verdienen
freckle ['frekl] Sonnensprosse
(to) **freeze to death** [fri:z]
    erfrieren
frilly ['frɪli] gekräuselt
front step [ˌfrʌnt 'step]
    Eingangsstufe
fun [fʌn]: (to) **make fun of sb.** sich
    über jn. lustig machen
fur [fɜ:] Fell
    furry pelzig
furious ['fjʊəriəs] wütend; wild
fuzzy [fʌzi] wuschelig

G
gentle ['dʒentl] sanft
Georgia ['dʒɔ:dʒə] *Staat im Süden*
    der USA
get [get]:
    1. (to) **get along** sich (gut)
    verstehen
    (to) **get beat** *(infml)* =
    get beaten besiegt werden
    (to) **get mad at sb.** auf jn.
    wütend sein
    (to) **get over sb./sth.** über
    jn./etwas hinwegkommen
    2. **Get lost!** *(infml)* Hau(t) ab!
gift [gɪft] Geschenk; Talent
give [gɪv]: (to) **give in** nachgeben
    (to) **give up** aufgeben

glad [glæd] froh
(to) **glow** [gləʊ] leuchten
go [gəʊ]: (to) **go about doing sth.**
    etwas in Angriff nehmen
    (to) **go off** (to) sich
    aufmachen (zu)
    (to) **go on sb.** *(infml) hier:*
    schlechter werden, nachlassen
    (to) **go with** passen zu
gone [gɒn]: **Be gone!** Geh weg!
Good grief! [ˌgʊd 'gri:f] Meine
    Güte!
gotta ['gɒtə] = **have got to**
grab [græb]: (to) **grab (hold of)**
    sb./sth. jn./etwas greifen/
    festhalten
grand [grænd] großartig
(to) **grin** [grɪn] grinsen
grocery store ['grəʊsəri: ˌstɔ:]
    (AE) Supermarkt
(to) **grow up** [ˌgrəʊ_'ʌp]
    erwachsen werden; wachsen
(to) **growl** [graʊl] knurren
grown-up ['grəʊnʌp] erwachsen;
    Erwachsene/r
guess [ges]: **I should have**
    guessed. Ich hätte es mir
    denken können.
gulp [gʌlp]: **in one big gulp** mit
    einem Bissen

H
handcuffs *(pl)* ['hændkʌfs]
    Handschellen
handsome ['hænsəm]
    gutaussehend
happiness ['hæpɪnəs]
    Glück(seligkeit)

hard [hɑːd] streng
hardly ['hɑːdli] kaum
harsh [hɑːʃ] streng
head [hed]:
1. (to) **head back** sich auf den Rückweg machen
2. **head start** Vorsprung
she cocked her head sie neigte den Kopf
not make head or tail of sth. mit etwas nichts anfangen können
healthy ['helθi] gesund
hell [hel] Hölle
hem [hem] Saum
hero ['hɪərəʊ] Held
high-heeled [ˌhaɪ'hiːld] mit hohen Absätzen
hind leg [ˌhaind 'leg] Hinterbein
(to) **hiss** [hɪs] zischen
(to) **hog sth.** [hɒg] etwas in Beschlag nehmen
hold [həʊld]: (to) **hold on tight to sb./sth.** jn./etwas festhalten/umarmen
(to) **holler** ['hɒlə] rufen
hose [həʊz] Wasserschlauch
(to) **howl** [haʊl] heulen *(bei Tieren)*
huge [hjuːdʒ] riesig
(to) **hum** [hʌm] summen
humour ['hjuːmə]: **sense of humour** Sinn für Humor
hunch [hʌntʃ]: **he hunched up his shoulders** er zog die Schultern hoch
hunting dog ['hʌntɪŋ ˌdɒg] Jagdhund

hymn [hɪm] Hymne

I
idle ['aɪdl] *hier:* beiläufig
ignorant ['ɪgnərənt] unwissend, dumm
immediately [ɪ'miːdiətli] sofort
inch [ɪntʃ] = Zoll (2,54 cm)
ingredient [ɪn'griːdiənt] Bestandteil, Zutat
instalment plan [ɪn'stɔːlmənt ˌplæn] Ratenzahlung
insulted [ɪn'sʌltɪd] beleidigt
(to) **intend** [ɪn'tend] beabsichtigen, vorhaben
(to) **introduce** [ˌɪntrə'djuːs] bekannt machen (mit)
(to) **invent** [ɪn'vent] erfinden
irritating ['ɪrɪteɪtɪŋ] nervig
itchy ['ɪtʃi] juckend, kratzend

J
jail [dʒeɪl] Gefängnis
jar [dʒɑː] Einmachglas
(to) **judge** [dʒʌdʒ] beurteilen

K
(to) **keep** [kiːp] behalten
(to) **keep sb. company** jm. Gesellschaft leisten
(to) **keep sb. safe** jn. beschützen
(to) **keep on doing sth.** fortfahren, etwas zu tun
kind [kaɪnd]: **kind of like** *(infml)* ungefähr so wie

knock [nɒk]: (to) **knock off**
umhauen (to) **knock sb. out**
jn. niederschlagen
(to) **knock sb./sth. over**
jn./etwas umwerfen
know [nəʊ]: (to) **know sb./sth.**
inside out jn./etwas in- und
auswendig kennen
know-it-all [ˈnəʊɪtɔːl]
Besserwisser
knuckle [nʌkl] (Finger)Knöchel

L
lap [læp] Schoß
law [lɔː] Gesetz
(to) **break the law** gegen das
Gesetz verstoßen
(to) **lay off** [ˌleɪ_ˈɒf] aufhören
leaf [liːf] Blatt
(to) **lean** [liːn] beugen
(to) **leap** [liːp] springen
leash [liːʃ] Leine
leave [liːv]: (to) **leave sth. behind**
etwas zurücklassen
left [ˈleft]: (to) **be left out of sth.**
von etwas ausgeschlossen
werden
leftover [ˈleftəʊvə]
übrig(geblieben)
let [let]: (to) **let sb. go** jn. gehen
lassen (to) **let up** *(infml)*
nachlassen
(to) **lick** [lɪk] lecken
lie [laɪ] Lüge
light [laɪt]: (to) **light, lit, lit**
anzünden (to) **light up**
erleuchten
lightning [ˈlaɪtnɪŋ] Blitz

(to) **limp** [lɪmp] hinken
lizard [ˈlɪzəd] Eidechse
locked [ˈlɒkd]: (to) **be locked up**
eingesperrt sein
look [lʊk]: (to) **look off in a**
different direction in eine
andere Richtung schauen
loose [luːs] lose, locker
lose [luːz]: (to) **lose one's nerve**
den Mut verlieren
(to) **be lost** verloren sein
loser [luːzə] Verlierer/in
sore loser schlechte/r
Verlierer/in
louse [laʊs] *pl* lice [laɪs] Laus
(to) **lower** [ˈləʊə] senken
lozenge [ˈlɒzɪndʒ] Lutschbonbon,
Halsbonbon

M
magic [ˈmædʒɪk]: **Is that man**
magic? Kann der Mann
zaubern?
(to) **manufacture** [ˌmænjuˈfæktʃə]
herstellen
matching [ˈmætʃɪŋ] passend
matted-up [ˌmætɪd_ˈʌp] verfilzt
matter [ˈmætə]: it didn't **matter**
es machte nichts
mean [miːn] gemein
meantime [ˈmiːntaɪm]: **in the**
meantime in der Zwischenzeit
melancholy [ˈmelənkəli]
Melancholie, Schwermut
(to) **melt** [melt] *hier:* weich
werden
(to) **memorize** [ˈmeməraɪz] sich
etwas einprägen

(to) **mention** ['menʃn] erwähnen
mess [mes]: (to) **mess sth. up**
   etwas verderben
   You're a mess. *(infml)* Du bist
   ja eine Katastrophe.
might [maɪt] könnte
mind [maɪnd]: **in my mind**
   in meinem Kopf
(to) **miss** [mɪs] vermissen
miss-smarty-pants
   [ˌmɪs 'smɑːtipents] *(AE)*
   Besserwisserin
missionary ['mɪʃənri]
   Missionar/in
mistake [mɪ'steɪk]:
   (to) **mistake sth. for sth.** etwas
   für etwas anderes halten
mood [muːd] Stimmung
mosquito [mɒs'kiːtəʊ] Mücke
moss [mɒs] Moos
(to) **mumble** ['mʌmbl] nuscheln
murderer ['mɜːdərə] Mörder
mutt [mʌt] *(infml)* Köter
(to) **mutter** ['mʌtə] murmeln
myth [mɪθ] Mythos

N
name tag ['neɪm tæg]
   Namensschild
naw [nɔː] *(infml)* nee, nein
neat [niːt] klasse, prima
need [niːd]: **need to know sth.**
   etwas wissen müssen
neighbourhood ['neɪbəhʊd]
   Nachbarschaft
neither ['naɪðə], [niːðə]: **neither
   (one) of you** keine/r von euch

nervouslike ['nɜːvəslaɪk] *(infml)*
   irgendwie nervös
notion ['nəʊʃn] Vorstellung, Idee
nowhere ['nəʊweə]: **out of
   nowhere** aus dem Nichts
nudge [nʌdʒ] Stupser

O
(to) **occur** [ə'kɜː] passieren
(to) **offer** ['ɒfə] anbieten
Open Arms Baptist Church *Name
   der Kirchengemeinde*
orphan ['ɔːfn] Waise
ought to ['ɔːt tə] sollte
overgrown [ˌəʊvə'grəʊn]
   zugewachsen
own [əʊn]: **on your own** allein,
   ohne Hilfe
owner ['əʊnə] Besitzer/in

P
palmetto [pæl'metəʊ]
   Palmettopalme
(to) **pant** [pænt] keuchen
pants [pænts] *(pl, AE)* Hose
past [pɑːst] vorbei
(to) **pat** [pæt] festklopfen
pat [pæt] Klaps
patch [pætʃ] Fleck
pathological [ˌpæθə'lɒdʒɪkl]
   krankhaft
peanut butter [ˌpiːnʌt 'bʌtə]
   Erdnussbutter
peculiar [pɪ'kjuːliə] eigenartig
pet [pet] Haustier
   1. **pet supplies** Haustierbedarf
   2. (to) **pet** streicheln
pew [pjuː] Kirchenbank

pick [pɪk]: (to) **pick a fight** einen
Streit provozieren
(to) **pick on sb.** jn. ärgern
(to) **pick out sth.** etwas
auswählen
(to) **pick sth. up** lernen
pickles ['pɪkls] saure Gurken,
eingelegtes Gemüse
pile [paɪl] Stapel
pinch-faced [ˌpɪntʃ'feɪst]
griesgrämig
pinched up [ˌpɪntʃt _ 'ʌp]
verkniffen
platter ['plætə] Platte, großer
Teller
plumb [plʌm] *(infml, AE)* total
point [pɔɪnt]: (to) **point sth. out**
auf etwas zeigen
pointy-toed [ˌpɔɪnti'təʊd] spitz
poke [pəʊk]: (to) **poke at sth.**
nach etwas stoßen
(to) **poke out** herausstrecken
polite [pə'laɪt] höflich
pop [pɒp]: (to) **pop out of sth.** aus
etwas heraustreten
porch [pɔːtʃ] Veranda
positive ['pɒzətɪv]: **Are you**
positive? Bist du sicher?
pot [pɒt] (Koch)topf
potion ['pəʊʃn] Zaubertrank
potluck supper [ˌpɒtlʌk 'sʌpə]
Essen, zu dem jeder Eingeladene
etwas mitbringt
pound [paʊnd] Tierheim
(to) **pour** [pɔː] (ein)gießen
prayer [preə] Gebet
preacher ['priːtʃə] Prediger
(to) **predict** [prɪ'dɪkt]
vorhersagen

(to) **pretend** [prɪ'tend]
vortäuschen
prideful ['praɪdfʊl] *(infml)*
hochmütig
probably ['prɒbəbli]
wahrscheinlich
produce section ['prɒdjuːs ˌsekʃn]
(AE) Lebensmittelabteilung
(to) **promise** ['prɒmɪs]
versprechen
properly ['prɒpəli] richtig,
ordentlich
(to) **protect** [prə'tekt] beschützen
proud [praʊd] stolz
punch [pʌntʃ] Punsch
pure [pjʊə] rein
purpose ['pɜːpəs]: **on purpose** mit
Absicht

Q

(to) **quit** [kwɪt] aufhören

R

(to) **race** [reɪs] um die Wette
laufen
railroad tracks ['reɪlrəʊd træks]
(pl, AE) Bahngleise
raise [reɪz]: (to) **raise** anheben
(to) **raise an eyebrow** die
Augenbraue hochziehen
(to) **reach (inside)** [riːtʃ] (hinein)
langen
reason ['riːzn] Grund
(to) **reason sb. out of sth.** jm.
etwas mit guten Gründen
ausreden
(to) **recall** [rɪ'kɔːl] sich erinnern
(to) **refresh** [rɪ'freʃ] erfrischen

regular ['regjələ] normal
relieved [rɪ'liːvd] erleichtert
remind [rɪ'maɪnd]: (to) **remind sb. of sth.** jn. an etwas erinnern
retarded [rɪ'tɑːdɪd] (geistig) zurückgeblieben
retriever [rɪ'triːvə] Retriever *(Hunderasse)*
ribbon ['rɪbən] (Haar)Band
right [raɪt] Recht
(to) **rock** [rɒk] *hier:* hin und her wiegen
root beer ['ruːt bɪə] Limonade aus Kräuter- oder Wurzelextrakten
rope [rəʊp] Seil
roundabout ['raʊndəbaʊt] umständlich
(to) **rub** [rʌb] reiben
rumble ['rʌmbl] Grollen, Poltern
run [rʌn]: (to) **run off** weglaufen
(to) **be/get run over** überfahren werden

S

(to) **scare** [skeə] erschrecken, Angst machen
(to) **scratch** [skrætʃ] kraulen
screechy ['skriːtʃi] kreischend
seen [siːn]: **I seen it/that.** *(infml)* Das habe ich gesehen.
select [sɪ'lekt] ausgewählte(r/s) **a select few** einige wenige Auserwählte
sensation [sen'seɪʃn] Gefühl
separated ['sepəreɪtɪd] getrennt
serious ['sɪəriəs] *hier:* feierlich
sermon ['sɜːmən] Predigt
(to) **serve** ['sɜːv] anbieten

set [set]: (to) **set sb. up on sth.** jm. etwas zur Verfügung stellen
shade [ʃeɪd] Schatten
(to) **shake** [ʃeɪk], **shook, shaken** schütteln; zittern
(to) **shame sb.** [ʃeɪm] jn. beschämen
(to) **share** [ʃeə] teilen **a share of sth.** (An)teil an
(to) **shave** [ʃeɪv] rasieren
shell [ʃel] Schale; Panzer *(bei Tieren)*
(to) **shine** [ʃaɪn], **shone, shone** scheinen
(to) **shrug** [ʃrʌg] mit den Schultern zucken
(to) **shuffle sth.** ['ʃʌfl] etwas hin- und herschieben
sidewalk ['saɪdwɔːk] *(AE)* Bürgersteig
(to) **sigh** [saɪ] seufzen
silk [sɪlk] Seide
(to) **skid** [skɪd] schlittern
skin [skɪn] Haut
skinny ['skɪni] schmal, dünn
(to) **slam** [slæm] (Tür) zuknallen; knallen
slavery ['sleɪvəri] Sklaverei
slick [slɪk]: **slicked back** mit Gel zurückgekämmt *(bei Haaren)*
(to) **slide** [slaɪd] gleiten
(to) **slither** ['slɪðə] sich schlängeln
smart [smɑːt] schlau
snake charmer ['sneɪk ˌtʃɑːmə] Schlangenbeschwörer/in
(to) **snatch sth. up** [snætʃ] etwas auffangen
(to) **sneak** [sniːk], **snuck, snuck** schleichen

(to) **snore** [snɔ:] schnarchen

(to) **snuffle** ['snʌfl] schnüffeln

soda ['səʊdə] Sprudelwasser

soldier ['səʊldʒə] Soldat/in

soon [su:n]: **as soon as** sobald

sore loser [ˌsɔ: 'lu:zə] schlechte/r Verlierer/in

sorrow ['sɒrəʊ] Sorge, Kummer

sorry ['sɒri]: **a sorry affair** eine traurige Sache

sound [saʊnd] Geräusch

specifically [spə'sɪfɪkli] besonders

spell [spel] Zauberspruch

(to) **spend** [spend] *hier:* verbringen

(to) **spit** [spɪt], **spat, spat** spucken

spooky ['spu:ki] unheimlich

spoonful ['spu:nfʊl] ein Löffel voll

(to) **spread** [spred] ausbreiten

(to) **squawk** [skwɔ:k] kreischen

(to) **squeeze** [skwi:z] drücken

(to) **squish** [skwɪʃ] *hier:* zerquetschen

stand [stænd]: **I can't stand ...** ich kann ... nicht ausstehen

(to) **stare at sth./sb.** [steə] etwas/jn. anstarren

(to) **start in (on doing sth.)** [stɑ:t] sich daranmachen (etwas zu tun)

stomach ['stʌmək] Magen

straight off [ˌstreɪt ˌ'ɒf] sofort

strange [streɪndʒ] eigenartig

stray [streɪ] streunender Hund

(to) **stretch** [stretʃ] sich strecken, räkeln

(to) **string** [strɪŋ], **strung, strung** aufhängen

string Schnur

(to) **strum** [strʌm] schrammeln, klimpern *(Gitarre)*

(to) **study** ['stʌdi] genau betrachten

stuff [stʌf]: (to) **stuff** (voll) stopfen

stuff *(infml)* Zeug; **... and stuff ...** und so

subject ['sʌbdʒekt] *hier:* Thema

(to) **suck** [sʌk] saugen, lutschen

sudden ['sʌdn]: **all of a sudden** ganz plötzlich

(to) **suffer** ['sʌfə] leiden

sugar ['sʊgə] *hier:* (meine) Süße *(Kosename)*

suit [su:t]: **Suit yourself.** Mach, was du willst.

sunflower seed ['sʌnflaʊə si:d] Sonnenblumenkern

supposed [sə'pəʊzd]: (to) **be supposed to do sth.** etwas tun sollen

surely ['ʃʊəli] gewiss, zweifellos

(to) **survive** [sə'vaɪv] überleben

(to) **sway** [sweɪ] schwanken

(to) **sweep** [swi:p] fegen

(to) **swell** [swel], **swelled, swollen** schwellen

(to) **swing** [swɪŋ], **swung, swung** schwingen

T

tail [teɪl]: **not make head or tail of sth.** mit etwas nichts anfangen können

tail light Rücklicht

(to) **talk sb. out of sth.** [tɔ:k] jn. von etwas abbringen

tank [tæŋk] Aquarium

(to) **tap** [tæp] klopfen; mit dem
Fuß wippen

tape [teɪp] Klebeband

(to) **tear** [teə], **tore, torn**
reißen; rasen

(to) **tease** [tiːz] necken; hänseln

teetery ['tiːtəri] schwankend

tell [tel]: (to) **tell on sb.** jn.
verraten/verpetzen
I could tell das merkte ich

though [ðəʊ] jedoch

throat [θrəʊt]: **he cleared his
throat** er räusperte sich

thumb [θʌm]: **green thumb**
grüner Daumen *(gut mit
Pflanzen umgehen können)*

(to) **thump** [θʌmp] heftig schlagen
thump dumpfer Plumps

thunderstorm ['θʌndəstɔːm]
Gewitter

tie [taɪ]: (to) **tie** (an)binden

tie [taɪ] Krawatte

tight [taɪt] fest

tile [taɪl] Fliese

tiny ['taɪni] sehr klein

toad [təʊd] Kröte

toothpick ['tuːθpɪk] Zahnstocher

top drawer [ˌtɒp 'drɔː] die oberste
Schublade

tragedy ['trædʒədi] Tragödie

trailer park ['treɪlə pɑːk]
Wohnwagensiedlung

treat [triːt]
1. besonderes Vergnügen
2. Genuss, Leckerei

(to) **tremble** ['trembl] zittern

triangle ['traɪæŋgl] Dreieck

(to) **trip over sth.** [trɪp] stolpern
über

trouble ['trʌbl]: (to) **be trouble**
Ärger machen

trustworthy ['trʌstwɜːði]
vertrauenswürdig

truth [truːθ] Wahrheit

(to) **tuck sb. (up) into bed** [tʌk]
jn. ins Bett stecken

turtle ['tɜːtl] Meeresschildkröte

Twelve Oaks ['twelv_əʊks] Zwölf
Eichen *(Plantagenname in
Gone With the Wind)*

(to) **twitch** [twɪtʃ] *hier:* (Ohren)
aufstellen

typhoid fever [ˌtaɪfɔɪd 'fiːvə]
Typhus

tyre ['taɪə] (Auto)Reifen

U

underneath [ˌʌndə'niːθ] unterhalb
(von)

unless [ən'les] wenn nicht

(to) **unwrap** [ʌn'ræp] auswickeln,
auspacken

(to) **upset** [ʌp'set] verärgern

V

vermin ['vɜːmɪn] Ungeziefer

vine [vaɪn] Kletterpflanze

Virginia [və'dʒɪniə] *Staat im Süden
der USA*

W

wad [wɒd] Bündel

wag [wæg]: (to) **wag the tail** mit
dem Schwanz wedeln

(to) **wail** [weɪl] wehklagen

War and Peace [ˌwɔːr_ənd_'piːs]
Krieg und Frieden (Roman von Leo Tolstoy)

(to) **wave** [weɪv] winken

way [weɪ]: **all the way up** bis obenhin
way past vorbei

(to) **wear sb. out** [weə] jn. ermüden

what [wɒt]: **what else** was noch; **what with** durch/dadurch, dass

(to) **wheeze** [wiːz] schnaufen, keuchen

(to) **whimper** ['wɪmpə] wimmern, winseln

(to) **whine** [waɪn] winseln

wife [waɪf] Ehefrau

(to) **wiggle** ['wɪgl] wackeln

wing [wɪŋ] Flügel

(to) **wink** [wɪŋk] zwinkern

(to) **wipe** [waɪp] wischen

witch [wɪtʃ] Hexe

(to) **wobble** ['wɒbl] wackeln

(to) **wonder** ['wʌndə] sich fragen

wore out [wɔː] *(infml)* = **worn out** erschöpft

world [wɜːld]: **the world over** auf der ganzen Welt

worth [wɜːθ]: **he ran for all he was worth** er rannte so schnell er konnte

would [wʊd]: **I wouldn't never** *(infml)* = **I would never**
Would you care for ...? Möchtest du ...?

wrap [ræp]: (to) **wrap one's arms around sb.** seine Arme um jn. legen

(to) **wrinkle** ['rɪŋkl] kräuseln

Y

Yankee ['jæŋki] *Soldat der Nordstaaten*

yappy dog ['jæpi dɒg] *(infml)* Kläffer

yard [jɑːd] *(AE)* Garten

(to) **yawn** [jɔːn] gähnen

years [jɪəz]: **in years** seit Jahren